John Franklin Jameson

The history of historical writing in America

John Franklin Jameson

The history of historical writing in America

ISBN/EAN: 9783337821319

Printed in Europe, USA, Canada, Australia, Japan

Cover: Foto ©ninafisch / pixelio.de

More available books at **www.hansebooks.com**

THE HISTORY OF HISTORICAL WRITING IN AMERICA

BY

J. FRANKLIN JAMESON, Ph. D.
PROFESSOR OF HISTORY IN BROWN UNIVERSITY

BOSTON AND NEW YORK
HOUGHTON, MIFFLIN AND COMPANY
The Riverside Press, Cambridge
1891

Copyright, 1891,
By J. FRANKLIN JAMESON.

All rights reserved.

The Riverside Press, Cambridge, Mass., U. S. A.
Printed by H. O. Houghton & Company.

PREFACE

THESE four Lectures upon the history of historical writing in America were read before public audiences in the hall of the Johns Hopkins University in January and February, 1887, and in that of Brown University in February and March, 1889. The third and fourth were printed in *Englische Studien* in 1888 and 1889, and the four, after a considerable revision, appeared in the *New England Magazine* in 1891.

BROWN UNIVERSITY, PROVIDENCE
May 2, 1891

CONTENTS

		PAGE
I.	THE HISTORIANS OF THE SEVENTEENTH CENTURY	1
II.	THE HISTORIANS OF THE EIGHTEENTH CENTURY	42
III.	FROM THE REVOLUTION TO THE CIVIL WAR	80
IV.	SINCE THE CIVIL WAR	122

THE HISTORY OF HISTORICAL WRITING IN AMERICA.

I.

THE HISTORIANS OF THE SEVENTEENTH CENTURY.

THE history of historical writing in the English colonies and in the United States falls, naturally, into four periods; and this alike whether we take as the basis of our classification its characteristics as historical literature, or its characteristics as historical science. In the first period, the heroic age of discovery and settlement, such history as we have is the work of the Argonauts themselves, who, with little consciousness of authorship, still less of membership in a literary profession, wrote down, in simplicity of mind, accounts of things which they had seen and in which they had themselves borne a great part. This period is roughly equivalent to the seventeenth century. Upon this followed two or three generations of what we might call epigonal historiography, bearing clear marks of a colonial or provincial origin, yet often careful and scholarly, and mainly devoted to investigating and recording with pious care the achievements of those who had preceded. The third period, lasting from the Revolution to the Civil War, was one in which history shared, in common with other departments, the effects of the general effort toward the creation of an independent American literature. During this, the classical period of our historical writing, the favorite subjects were portions of European history. Since then we have had a marked improvement in method and scholarship; but the dominant impulse of the fourth period has been toward a closer, and especially a broader, study of our own history. It is with these four periods that the chapters of this book are respectively to be occupied. In general, only the most important writers of each will be considered; and no effort will be made to relate at length the picturesque and interesting details of these writers' lives, — not from any such disdain of the picturesque as modern students of history are supposed to affect, but because the subject is not the lives and personalities of American historians, but the development of American historiography.

In the time of the first adventurers and settlers, some historical literature of value had already been produced by the nation from which they sprang, — chronicles like those of Hall and Holinshed, collections like those of Stow, and a few more notable performances, Lord Bacon's "Henry VII.," Knollys' "Historie of the Turkes," Fox's "Martyrs," and the great fragment of a "History of the World" which Raleigh had composed during his long imprisonment in the Tower. But no one of these was in any way the model of our earliest historians, whose purposes were quite different. The purpose of one class was to awaken immediate interest in a given colony, and stimulate immigration into it by accounts of what had been done there; to this class belong Captain John Smith and Captain Edward Johnson. The model of some of them may be seen in the pages of Hakluyt, in the Relations and Narratives of voyagers. The other class, of which Governor Bradford and

Governor Winthrop are the chief examples, believing themselves to have been concerned in memorable beginnings, wrote for the benefit of posterity permanent memorials, which they did not intend to be published till after their deaths. It is to these four, as best deserving, among our writers of the seventeenth century, the name of historian, that the present chapter is to be mainly given.

At the beginning at once of our colonial history and of American historical literature stands the burly figure of Captain John Smith; and yet he stands somewhat apart from both. There is no need to recount at length the stirring events of his early life, — how, after wandering over much of Europe and the Levant, he took service against the Turk, slew three Turkish cavaliers in single combat before the walls of Regall, was captured and sold as a slave, was befriended by a noble lady at Constantinople, was sent to serve as a slave in Crim-Tartary, and escaped with many adventures; but it is plain, from the nature of them, that he belonged in character to the generation that had just passed away. He had more in common with Hawkins and

Frobisher and Drake, with those who repulsed the Armada, and sought Eldorado, and braved the northern ice, and " singed the King of Spain's beard," with all the freshness and buoyancy and adventurousness of the Elizabethans, than with Eliot and Pym and Selden, with the sobriety, the seriousness, the prosaic strenuousness, which had begun to overspread and to characterize the England of James I. It was these traits of character that made him really unsuited to much of the work which now needed to be done in the American settlements. He was a colonial adventurer in a generation of colonial founders. At the beginning, the services of such a man were invaluable, and the colony probably owed more to him than to any other man during the thirty months that he spent in it. But, the initial work once done, another sort of talent was needed if the colony was to be, not abortive, as the Elizabethan colonial experiments had been, but a strong and prosperous community, founded on sober and humdrum agriculture and trade; and so the shrewd London merchants of the Virginia Company were not wrong in making no further use of Smith.

The same qualities shine conspicuous in

the writings of Smith, and mark him off from the rest as, though the precursor, yet not the father of the American historical writers. His writings breathe the spirit that invests the pages of Hakluyt and Purchas with so surpassing and so imperishable a charm, not that which has made our colonial history dull and our nation great. He writes, by preference, of encounters, of explorations, of opportunities for present gain, as one who is directing a band of adventurers, not as one who is thoughtfully laying foundations for the gradual growth of a mighty state. He does not lack seriousness, but he is more a knight-errant than a man of business. But if both his rôle and his attitude are those of a knight-errant, bearing in his veins the enthusiastic blood of the sixteenth century, but set to do the sober tasks of the seventeenth, he was in the main a worthy knight, fearing God after the simple, untroubled fashion of the earlier time, without overmuch sojourning in Meshec and Kedar, serving faithfully and energetically his king and the company, giving good government, and doing with his might what his hand found to do. He wrote of all this with keen zest and enjoyment, and with not too much of modesty, or of mildness toward his adversaries; but when was a knight-errant ever modest or conciliatory?

The strictly historical works of Captain John Smith are but two in number. The first is a brief tract of thirty or forty pages, entitled "A True Relation of such occurrences and accidents of noate as hath happned in Virginia since the first planting of that Collony, which is now resident in the South part thereof, till the last returne from thence." The second is the extensive book entitled "The Generall Historie of Virginia, New-England, and the Summer Isles," a brief continuation of which was printed as part second of his "True Travels, Adventures, and Observations." His other books are mostly of a descriptive character: they have a value as historical material; they are not themselves historical writings. The "True Relation" was written in Virginia about the end of May, 1608, when the colony had been in existence a little more than a year; it was sent home by Captain Nelson in the Phœnix, and was published at London in August. It is only a pamphlet, and a somewhat hastily prepared one at that. It is mainly occupied with the personal adventures of Smith himself, the exploring expeditions which he conducted, and his dealings with the Indians. Not much is told us of events at Jamestown. While that little is valuable, in the paucity of eye-witness accounts of the first year's doings, its value is much diminished, or at least rendered doubtful, by the fact that it is everywhere seen to be colored by Smith's hostility to certain fellow-members of the Council. Which was right in their frequent quarrels is hard now to determine; but no one can fail to see that Smith was too censorious of the actions of others, too vain of his own, to be a historical witness of the highest degree of merit.

The same animosities are to be found, unallayed after a period of sixteen years, in the "Generall Historie," published in 1620, the book which forms Smith's chief title to be numbered among the American historians. Or rather, it exhibits these animosities widened into partisanship in a more important conflict, and applied to the events of a greater number of years. Coming home in 1609, and never afterward succeeding in getting employment from the company, Smith seems to have extended his resentment againt those who had ruled the colony with him to their successors, and eventually to the managers of the company. In the last years of James I., the Virginia Company's proceedings reflected the conflict going on in the country at large, the minority being of the court party, the managers belonging to the opposition. Smith takes many opportunities in the "Generall Historie" to attack them, to accuse the mismanagement of the colony since he left it, and to lament that his advice was not rather followed and his services employed. "I know," he adds, "I shall be taxed for writing so much of my selfe; but I care not much, because the judiciall know there are few such Souldiers as [those who] have writ their owne actions, nor know I who will or can tell my intents better then my selfe."

The book which the doughty captain had prepared with so resolute a disregard of all natural impulses toward self-effacement was proposed, as the records of the Virginia Company show, as early as 1621, but published in 1624, in a volume of two hundred and fifty pages folio, embellished with several quaint and well-engraved maps. Smith was, after all, the author of only about seventy-five pages out of the two hundred and fifty; and of these seventy-five, nearly seventy comprise mere reprints from three of his descriptive books. Of all the rest he was but the editor or compiler. The composition of the book is in fact singular. The first book, treating of the English voyages to Virginia before 1607, is entirely a compilation or patchwork of previous narratives. The second book is a reprinted description of Virginia as it was in 1607. The third book is a republication, with some variations, of a body of narratives by some of the original planters, which had been edited by one Dr. Simonds, and published in 1612; they cover the thirty months of Smith's stay in the colony, and are from persons belonging to his faction. What he himself has contributed to this division is limited to the insertion, here and there, of verses more remarkable for sententiousness than for beauty, and, it must be added, the addition of striking adventures not mentioned in the "True Relation," and a general heightening of the picturesqueness of his own career. The fourth book, giving the history of Virginia from 1609 to 1624, is almost wholly a compilation, or rather a transcription, of the narratives of residents; the fifth, treating of the history of the Bermudas, is wholly so. Finally, to make Book VI., entitled "The Generall Historie of New England," he reprints his "Description of New England," 1616, and "New England's Trials," 1620, inserts Edward Winslow's "Plantation in New England," and, with a few interesting pages on the present estate of New Plymouth, closes this remarkable historical mosaic, of which it may almost be said that what is historical is not his, and what is his is not historical. But herein, also, we must confess, he has been the precursor of many of our historical writers, not all of whom have enumerated as frankly as he the victims of their scissors.

Nothing has been said, thus far, of the story of the saving of Smith by Pocahontas. The historical student who is not entirely steeped in haughty professionalism, who would himself "strictly meditate the thankless Muse," yet wishes to temper that austere cult with a regard for the unscientific preferences of Amaryllis and Neæra, will certainly hesitate long before assailing the most famous of the few romantic legends of our early colonial history. And yet it appears that, in spite of a dozen novels and perhaps a gross of poems, that have gathered about it, the legend must go. A whole chapter would hardly be long enough for a full discussion of the arguments, but in brief the case is this. Not only is there no mention of such an episode in the full account of his Chickahominy expedition which Smith gave, a few months after he went upon it, in the "True Relation," but everything there indicates a most friendly reception by Powhatan; nor do any of his companions mention an adventure so striking. It first appears in print in the "Generall Historie" of 1624, interpolated as one of those embellishments of his friends' accounts, to which allusion has been made. It appears that Smith, in 1616, hinted at such a service performed by Pocahontas, in a letter to the Queen, written when Pocahontas was in England. In short, the probability is that he invented the episode in order to connect himself in a picturesque manner with one who had lately been attracting so much attention. One need not stop to defend historical criticism for destroying so pretty a legend, for historical criticism brings to light two stories of heroism that are true where it removes one that is false; but perhaps we may more easily be reconciled to the loss of this particular romance if we remember that, pictures and poems and story-books to the contrary notwithstanding, the real Pocahontas was only ten years old at the time of the alleged rescue.

To turn from Captain John Smith to Governor William Bradford is like turning from "Amadis of Gaul" to the "Pilgrim's Progress." The worthy governor of Plymouth Plantation had slain no Turks, had undergone no romantic adventures, had been signally befriended by no princesses or noble dames, whether heathen, Mohammedan, or Christian. But if fortune denied him interesting adventures, — except in so far as the high purposes of the Pilgrim Fathers and the permanent importance of their work invest all that they did with interest, — it did not deal so with his book. The story of its vicissitudes is a curious one. It was well known to historical scholars that Governor Bradford had left behind him a manuscript history of Plymouth Plantation.

Some extracts from it had been given in print by certain historical writers of the hundred years succeeding his death, the last being Governor Hutchinson, in 1767. It was supposed that Bradford's descendants had lent it to the Rev. Thomas Prince, the noted historical scholar of Boston, and that Prince had deposited it in the New England Library which he was forming, in the tower of the Old South Church. During the first year of the Revolutionary War, while Boston was occupied by the British, that church was, as is well known, used by them as a riding-school. After that time, nothing was heard of the precious manuscript of Bradford's history, until, one day in 1855, a local antiquary most unexpectedly found a trace of it. While reading a small English book by Bishop Wilberforce on the history of the Protestant Episcopal Church in America, he came upon certain passages which were identical with some of the extracts from Bradford given, as already mentioned, by American writers of the last century. The foot-notes of the book described these passages as taken from a manuscript history of the Plantation of Plymouth, in the library of the Bishop of London at

Fulham. The discovery was communicated to one of the leading members of the Massachusetts Historical Society, and a correspondence was entered upon. The manuscript in the bishop's library was proved to be that of Governor Bradford's long-lost history, and was copied, and printed in 1856. How it came to be in the Fulham library no one knows; nor does any one know how to get it back from there.

However, we have the printed text, and a most important and interesting work it is. Governor Bradford's qualifications for preparing such a history are manifest. From the first year of the settlement down to the time of his death — during a period, that is, of thirty-six years — there had been but five years in which he had not been elected governor of the colony. He had been among the earlier fugitives to Holland, and was, therefore, personally cognizant of the history of the little community in the period preceding its transfer to America. During most of the long period of his governorship he had had in mind the preparation of such an account, of which it appears that he wrote the beginning in 1630, and the end in 1650, and had been saving and collecting letters and documents important to his purpose. He had, therefore, the most entire familiarity with the history of the colony, and time enough to insure deliberation and care. Moreover, he had not only a thoughtful mind and a high degree of intelligence, but was even, like so many of the early American governors, a man of some scholarship. Cotton Mather says of him : " He was a person for study as well as action; and hence, notwithstanding the difficulties through which he passed in his youth, he attained unto a notable skill in languages ; the Dutch tongue was become almost as vernacular to him as the English; the French tongue he could also manage ; the Latin and the Greek he had mastered; but the Hebrew he most of all studied, because, he said, he would see with his own eyes the ancient oracles of God in their native beauty. He was also well skilled in history, in antiquity, and in philosophy; and for theology, he became so versed in it that he was an irrefragable disputant against . . . errors. . . . But the crown of all was his holy, prayerful, watchful, and fruitful walk with God, wherein he was very exemplary." It may illustrate the cast of Bradford's mind to repeat what he himself has said in regard to one of these studies. Eight manuscript pages of Hebrew roots with English equivalents, and of Hebrew exercises, have been found, written in his handwriting, and prefaced with these remarks: "Though I am growne aged, yet I have had a longing desire to see, with my owne eyes, something of that most ancient language, and holy tongue, in which the law and oracles of God were writ; and in which God and angels spake to the holy patriarchs of old time; and what names were given to things, from the creation. And though I cannot attaine to much herein, yet I am refreshed to have seen some glimpse hereof (as Moyses saw the land of Canan afarr of). My aim and desire is, to see how the words and phrases lye in the holy texte; and to discerne somewhat of the same, for my owne contente."

But whatever scholarship the excellent governor may have had, he does not obtrude it into his book, which has nothing of the pedantic manner so frequent in the seventeenth century. He writes a plain, sober, and straightforward account, the evident care and accuracy of which make it one of the most valued sources for our colonial period. His narrative covers the history of the colony down to the year 1646, at which point it was left unfinished. It embraces the events which led, in England and Holland, to the exodus of the Pilgrims, the now familiar tale of their early sufferings and achievements, the occasional controversies in which they were involved, their negotiations with other colonies, their troubles with the London merchants, and their correspondence and relations with the body whom they had left behind at their departure. The phrases in which that departure is described are memorable: "So they lefte that goodly and pleasante citie, which had been ther resting place near twelve years; but they knew they were pilgrimes, and looked not much on those things, but lift up their eyes to the heavens, their dearest countrie, and quieted their spirits." Such words as these, which have been often quoted, do not stand alone in the narrative; with all its sobriety, it is clothed in many passages with that exquisite and singular beauty of expression which a close familiarity with the English translation of the Bible has so often bestowed on writers of little literary art. Of such is the following, written in appreciative commemoration of his companions' fortitude.

"But hear," he says, "I cannot but stay and make a pause, and stand half amased at this poore peoples presente condition; and so I thinke will the reader, too, when he well considers the same. Being thus past the vast ocean, and a sea of troubles before in their preparation, . . . they had now no friends to welcome them nor inns to entertaine or refresh their weatherbeaten bodys, no houses or much less townes to repair too, to seeke for succoure. It is recorded in scripture as a mercie to the apostle & his shipwraked company, that the barbarians shewed them no smale kindnes in refreshing them, but these savage barbarians, when they mette with them, . . . were readier to fill their sids full of arrows then otherwise. And for the season it was winter, and they that know the winters of that cuntrie know them to be sharp and violent, and subjecte to cruell and feirce stormes, deangerous to travill to known places, much more to serch an unknown coast. Besids, what could they see but a hidious and desolate wildernes, full of wild beasts and willd men? And what multituds ther might be of them they knew not. Nether could they, as it were, goe up to the tope of Pisgah, to vew from this willdernes a more goodly cuntrie to feed their hops; for which way soever they turned their eys (save upward to the heavens) they could have litle solace or content in respecte of any outward objects. . . . Let it also be considered what weake hopes of supply and succoure they left behind them, that might bear up their minds in this sade condition and trialls they were under. . . . What could now sustaine them but the spirite of God and his grace? May not and ought not the children of these fathers rightly say: Our faithers were Englishmen which came over this great ocean, and were ready to perish in this willdernes; but they cried unto the Lord, and he heard their voyce, and looked on their adversitie, &c. Let them, therefore, praise the Lord, because he is good, and his mercies endure forever. Yea, let them which have been redeemed of the Lord, shew how he hath delivered them from the hand of the oppressour. When they wandered in the desert willdernes out of the way, and found no citie to dwell in, both hungrie and thirstie, their sowle was overwhelmed in them. Let them confess before the Lord his loving kindnes, and his wonderful works before the sons of men."

It is a curious good fortune by which we happen to have accounts of two of our earliest colonies, those of Plymouth and of Massachusetts Bay, written by the two men who had most to do with managing the affairs of each in the earliest period. Moreover, the two governors and historians were in some degree typical of the two colonies whose history they helped to make and to write. The Separatist colony and the Puritan colony were widely different. The history of the Pilgrim Fathers is full of suffering, of poverty, of humility, of patience, and of mildness. It is the story of a small and feeble enterprise, glorified by faith and hope and charity, but necessarily and always limited by the slender resources of the poor and humble men who originated it. The founding of the Bay colony, on the other hand, was less a colonial enterprise than a great Puritan emigration. It was organized by men of substance and standing, supported by the wealth of a great and prosperous body of the English nation, and consciously directed toward the high end of founding in America a great Puritan state. And as Massachusetts was to Plymouth Plantation, so, in many respects, was Governor John

Winthrop to Governor William Bradford. He was, in the first place, a man of much more prominent position, lord of the manor of Groton, one of the attorneys of the Court of Wards and Liveries, a magistrate, and a man of considerable wealth. But he was also a man of a broader, larger, and more philosophic intellect, as well as of a more regular and extensive education. In short, he had more thoroughly those powers and acquisitions of mind which would fit one to direct worthily the larger concerns of a strong and important state, and to describe worthily its origin and early development. For beauty of character, it is hard to give the preference to either governor. Long possession of great power in a community resolute to defend its independence and suppress dissension with a high hand, strong, self-reliant, and intolerant, never succeeded in marring the exquisite sensitiveness of Winthrop's conscience, or affecting the gentleness and sweetness of his deportment. Scrupulosity of conscience we perhaps expect to find in a Puritan, but the second point is worth a little more attention. It is worth while frequently to insist that harshness, and sourness, and gloom were not characteristic of all periods of Puritan history alike. Puritanism in New England, as in Old England, went through three different stages, — the period of origin and growth, the period of conflict, the period of decline. The Puritanism which was satirized in "Hudibras," and which fell with Richard Cromwell, was not the Puritanism of the civil wars. Still less was it the Puritanism of Milton's earlier years, — of "Comus" and "L'Allegro" and "Il Penseroso." In that earlier time, Puritanism had not dissevered itself from the cheerfulness and spontaneity of the Elizabethan period, but had simply added to them, on the one hand a greater degree of moral earnestness, and on the other hand a greater zeal for innovation in church and state. So it was in New England. The well-known and most amusing diary of Chief Justice Sewall shows us Puritanism as it had come to be among the men of the third generation, — Puritanism gone to seed, grown narrow and harsh and petty, and rapidly becoming mundane and Philistine. But before this, and before the preceding generation of conflict, and before the hardships of life and the wildness of nature had begun to depress men's minds to the level of the awful righteousness with which we are so familiar, there was a Puritanism of a less unlovely type; serious and strict, but not uncheerful, nor insensible to the delights and beauty of life. Of such Puritanism John Winthrop was the type and the exponent. In him Puritanism is seen at its best, not only caring (and compelling others to care) for what was in its opinion true and honest and just, but also observant of whatsoever things are lovely and of good report. The poetic imagination which led him to prefer, of all books of the Bible, the Song of Solomon, the depth and beauty of his religious experiences, the exquisite tenderness of his letters to his wife, the mildness of his efficient rule as governor, all show us a nature singularly attractive. He was, in short, a gentleman; not in the spurious sense of one whose ancestors and connections have been highly distinguished for being related to each other, but in the better sense of one who combines with a noble character the additional graces of a perfect sweetness of temper and a perfect refinement of manner.

I have enlarged upon Winthrop's personal characteristics because they were an important factor in the composition of his book. Of a historian of our day, writing of these things, this need not be true. But in the case of one who writes of the genesis of a state of which he has been the foremost founder, the study of his personality is a matter of much consequence to the critic, not only because it helps to understand his book, but also because it helps to understand the movement which he headed. Milton, in a famous passage of the Apology for Smectymnuus, reminds us "that he who would not be frustrate of his hope to write well hereafter in laudable things, ought himself to be a true poem, . . . not presuming to sing high praises of heroic men or famous cities, unless he have in himself the experience and the practice of all that which is praiseworthy." John Winthrop did have within himself these things. They shone out plainly in the acts of his public life, and they are not less conspicuous in the history which he left behind him.

The "History of New England" has the form of annals, or even, at first, of a journal, begun by the governor on board the Arbella on the day when he set sail from England in 1630. It is continued to the winter of 1648, a few months before his death. Naturally, many matters of small moment are treated in it, — minor doings of the governing body and the churches, moving accidents, remarkable providences, and so forth. But the narrative is never undignified and never gossiping. And when events of greater importance to the colony, or deliberations and discussions involving the essential principles of its policy, fall to be described, we could hardly desire a guide more impartial, more informing, or more thoughtful. Together with the actions of the rulers their reasons are set before us, and set before us with a high-minded confidence and a philosophic breadth of view that leave nothing to be desired. Once in a while occur really admirable reasonings and statements in matters of political philosophy; while the absence of passion and intolerance and pettiness is very marked. The early years of the colony were a time of strong party feeling and of bitter dissensions; yet Winthrop never takes the opportunity of private writing and posthumous publication to set down aught in malice against any of his opponents. Of the chief among them, Sir Harry Vane, he says that at all times " he showed himself a true friend to New England, and a man of a noble and generous mind." The severest thing that he says of any of them, so far as I know, is found in some words of grave and temperate disapprobation which he uses with regard to Governor Bellingham, and even here he does not fail to suggest what excuse he can for Bellingham's factious ill-temper. Speaking in one passage of some of these disagreements, he says: "Indeed, it occasioned much grief to all the elders, and gave great offence through the country; and such as were acquainted with other states in the world, and had not well known the persons, would have concluded such a faction here as hath been usual in the council of England and other states, who walk by politic principles only. But these gentlemen were such as feared God, and endeavored to walk by the rules of his word in all their proceedings, so as it might be conceived in charity that they walked according to their judgments and conscience, and where they went aside it was merely for want of light, or their eyes were held through some temptation for a time, that they could not make use of the light they had; for in all these differences and agitations about them, they continued in brotherly love, and in the exercise of all friendly offices each to other, as occasion required." And the story of the governor's own reconciliation with Dudley shows that, so far as he himself was concerned, he has not overstated the case.

Winthrop's narrative, like Bradford's, was left in manuscript at his death, and came to be a part of the New England Library in the Old South Church. Its subsequent vicissitudes were curious, though not so remarkable as those of the "History of Plymouth Plantation." After the Revolution, two of the three volumes of the manuscript were found in the possession of the elder branch of the Winthrops in Connecticut, edited, very superficially it must be said, by the redoubtable lexicographer, Noah Webster, and published in 1790. In 1816, the third volume was discovered in the dormitory of the Old South Church. The Massachusetts Historical Society entrusted the preparation of a new edition of the whole to James Savage. Before he had accomplished the collation of the second volume of the manuscript, that volume was destroyed by a fire which broke out in his office. The first and the third volumes are now in the library of the society; for the second, our text is that of Webster's edition.

He who is seeking a characteristic production of the traditional Puritan should without doubt resort to that of the fourth and last writer upon our list. Its very title is characteristically Puritan. It was an age of quaint title-pages; but nowhere were they quainter than in the books of the New England Puritans. "New England's Teares for Old England's Feares," "New England's Salamander Discovered," "New England's Jonas cast up at London," "The Heart of New England rent at the Blasphemies of the Present Generation," and, for a longer example, that of John Cotton's famous pamphlet, "Milk for Babes, drawn out of the Breasts of both Testaments, chiefly for the Spiritual Nourishment of Boston Babes, but may be of like use to other Children,"— such are the names of some of the early historical and controversial tracts of New England. Among them all, few have a quainter title than that which the author of the historical book before us bestowed upon it, — "The Wonder-Working Providence of Sion's Saviour in New England." The London publisher saw fit to alter this upon the title-page to "The History of New England;" but in the head-lines of the pages the title chosen by the author is followed throughout. A history of New England the book is not, but rather a history of Massachusetts down to the year 1651. Among the New England histories it has the distinction of having been the first to appear in print, for it was printed in London in 1653 (dated 1654). It was printed anonymously, but its author is known to have been Captain Edward Johnson, selectman and town clerk of the town of Woburn in Massachusetts. In Governor Winthrop, as I have declared, we may see Puritanism at its very best. But the *élite* of humanity are nowhere in a majority. A better representative of the average Puritan of the middle class is doubtless Captain Johnson. He was a Kentish farmer, and probably also a shipwright, who came out in the same fleet with Winthrop in 1630. A dozen years later, he was, in company with half a dozen others, one of the founders of the new town of Woburn. It is interesting to note that, of his dozen companions in this undertaking, one, John Sedgwick, afterward became one of Cromwell's major-generals, while another rose in the naval service of

England to be Rear-Admiral Thomas Graves. But the stout Kentishman, having put his hand to the plough, chose to remain in the town he had helped to plant. He had always an important part in the affairs of the town, was chosen selectman nearly every year, was again and again elected to represent the town in the general court or legislature of the colony, acted as town clerk, and was captain of the train-band. He was, therefore, more or less concerned in the public affairs in the colony, but never had a leading part in them. Though he was a more prominent, a wealthier, and perhaps a more intelligent man than most of his fellow-citizens, we may well enough take him as in most respects a type of the rank and file of the original settlers. This is in the main what gives its value to this first printed history of Massachusetts.

Captain Edward Johnson was far inferior to Governor Winthrop in breadth, in culture, and in fineness of spirit. The hot zeal, the narrow partisanship, the confident dogmatism, which characterized so much of Puritanism, have in him a striking example. No one could be more remote from the cool, skeptical, examining temper of the modern historian, who hears, and smiles, and deducts, and balances. All Johnson's opinions are self-evident to him. He sees no good in the lords bishops. He will not listen to the servants of the chief priests; rather, his first impulse is to draw a sword and cut off Malchus' ear. He is full of that narrow Hebraism which, when it prayed, kept open its windows toward Jerusalem, but closed every other avenue to the soul. To hew Agag in pieces before the Lord is to his mind not the least attractive of religious duties. With him the church militant is more than a metaphor. The life of the colony appears to him most frequently in the guise of an armed conflict; he hears in its story the noise of battle, the thunder of the captains and the shouting, and in vehement canticles summons the Israel of New England to the help of the Lord against the mighty. Old Testament phrases are his delight; he speaks, throughout, the dialect which the French wittily call the *patois de Canaan*. To the Puritan zeal he adds the Puritan superstition. Everywhere the hand of the Lord is seen protecting his saints; his wonder-working Providence appears not only in the general movement of the events narrated, but in every detail of the fortunes and misfortunes of individuals, so that his pages bristle with special providences. His account of one of these may be quoted: —

"To end this yeare 1639, the Lord was pleased to send a very sharp winter, and more especially in strong storms of weekly snows, with very bitter blasts; And here the Reader may take notice of the sad hand of the Lord against two persons, who were taken in a storme of snow, as they were passing from Boston to Roxbury, it being much about a mile distant, and a very plaine way. One of Roxbury sending to Boston his servant maid for a Barber-Chirurgion to draw his tooth, they lost their way in their passage between, and were not found till many dayes after, and then the maid was found in one place, and the man in another, both of them frozen to death; in which sad accident, this was taken into consideration by divers people, that this barber was more than ordinary laborious to draw men to those sinfull Errors, that were formerly so frequent, and now newly overthrowne by the blessing of the Lord, ... he having a fit opportunity, by reason of his trade, so soone as they were set downe in his chaire, he would commonly be cutting of their haire and the truth together; notwithstanding some report better of the man, the example is for the living, the dead is judged of the Lord alone."

This last is a redeeming touch. It cannot be said that it is not in some degree characteristic. With all the illiberality and harshness of his theological zeal, the man was not unkindly. Something of the spirit of Winthrop appeared in even the less enlightened of those who followed him; Johnson's Puritanism was not all unlovely, and at any rate it was far from ignoble. Let us be just to the Puritans. Doubtless they would not be agreeable neighbors. Doubtless they would have hanged or burned a considerable number of us, and banished all the rest; for in these degenerate days hardly any one is orthodox according to their standards. Yet let us remember that they did possess, in an eminent degree, those virtues that spring from confidence in a high purpose and a mission felt to be momentous and sacred, from belief in character, from belief in enthusiasm, from belief in strenuous effort. If the bit of quaint superstition which has been quoted is characteristic of Johnson and his companions, not less characteristic is the following passage, in which is exhibited in an instructive manner the attitude of the struggling colony toward its cherished college. Describing the eager desire of the colonists that learning should be adequately maintained among them, he says: "And verily had not the Lord been pleased to furnish N. E. with means for the attainment of learning, the work would have been carried on very heavily, and the hearts of godly parents would have vanish'd away with heaviness for their poor children, whom they must have left in a desolate wilderness, destitute of the meanes of grace." After picturesquely setting forth their sense of the magnitude of such an enterprise as the foundation of a college in comparison with their feeble resources, he goes on to say: —

"Hereupon all those who had tasted the sweet wine of Wisdom's drawing, and fed on the dainties of knowledg, began to set their wits a work. . . . Means they know there are, many thousands uneyed of mortal man, which every daies Providence brings forth; upon these resolutions, to work they go, and with thankful acknowledgement, readily take up all lawful means as they come to hand, for place they fix their eye upon New Town, which to tell their Posterity whence they came, is now named Cambridg, and withal to make the whole world understand, that spiritual learning was the thing they chiefly desired, to sanctifie the other, and make the whole lump holy, and that learning being set upon its right object, might not contend for error instead of truth; they chose this place, being then under the Orthodox, and soul-flourishing Ministry of Mr. Thomas Shepheard. . . . The scituation of this colleg is very pleasant, at the end of a spacious plain, more like a bowling-green, then a wilderness, neer a fair navigable river, environed with many Neighboring Towns of note, . . . the building thought by some to be too gorgeous for a wilderness, and yet too mean in others apprehensions for a colleg, it is at present inlarging by purchase of the neighbour houses, it hath the conveniences of a fair Hall, comfortable Studies, and a good Library, given by the liberal hand of some Magistrates and Ministers with others. The chief gift towards the founding of this Colledg, was by Mr. John Harvard, a reverend Minister; the country being very weak in their publike

Treasury, expended about 500. £ toward it, and for the maintenance thereof, gave the yearly revenue of a Ferry passage between Boston and Charlestown, the which amounts to about 40. or 50. £ per annum. . . . This Colledg hath brought forth, and nurst up very hopeful plants, to the supplying some churches here, as the gracious and godly Mr. Wilson, son to the grave and zealous servant of Christ, Mr. John Wilson, [and others]. . . . Mr. Henry Dunster is now president of [it], fitted from the Lord for the work, and by those that have skill that way reported to be an able Proficient, in both Hebrew, Greek, and Latine languages, an Orthodox preacher of the truths of Christ, very powerful through his blessing to move the affection; and besides he having a good inspection into the well-ordering of things for the Students' maintenance (whose commons hath been very short hitherto) by his frugal providence hath continued them longer at their studies than otherwise they could have done; and, verily, it's great pity such ripe heads as many of of them be, should want means to further them in learning."

One curious feature of Johnson's style of

historical composition remains to be noted. This is his habit of inserting in his narrative bits of original verse. The earliest colonial writers were somewhat addicted to this habit. Roger Williams closes each short chapter of his Indian grammar, or "Key into the Language of America," with a stanza or so of verses as bad as any that one often encounters; John Smith, we have seen, developed in later life something of this habit. But few among them all had it in a more aggravated form than the author of the "Wonder-Working Providence." His book contains no less than sixty-eight poems. The present writer has read them all, with the pious care of a lineal descendant, and can confidently state that they are all very bad. One of them, on the Massachusetts Company, runs in this unconsciously brisk and jaunty manner:

"For richest Jems and gainfull things most Merchants
    wisely venter;
Deride not then New England men, this Corporation
    enter;
Christ calls for Trade shall never fade, come Craddock
    factors send;
Let Mayhew go and other more, spare not thy coyne to
    spend;
Such Trades advance did never chance, in all thy Trading
    yet,
Though some deride thy losse, abide, her's gaine beyond
    man's wit."

Most of them, however, are in honor or commemoration of individual persons prominently concerned in the foundation of the colony, or godly ministers of its churches. The author, after mentioning the person, inserts some modest introductory phrase, such as, "of whom the author is bold to say as followeth," or "in remembrance of whom mind this meeter," and then, to use a phrase now become classic, "drops into poetry." One of the most characteristic is that which ensues after the mention of Governor John Endicott. "And now," he says, "let no man be offended at the author's rude verse, penned of purpose to keepe in memory the names of such worthies as Christ made strong for himselfe, in this unwonted worke of his."

"Strong valiant John wilt thou march on, and take up station first,
Christ cal'd hath thee, his soldier be, and faile not of thy trust;
Wilderness wants Christ's grace supplants, then plant his Churches pure,
With Tongues gifted, and graces led, help thou to his procure;
Undaunted thou wilt not allow, Malignant men to wast:
Christs Vineyard heere, whose grace should cheere, his well-beloved's tast.
Then honoured be, thy Christ hath thee their Generall promoted:

> To show their love, in place above, his people have thee voted.
> Yet must thou fall, to grave with all the Nobles of the Earth,
> Thou rotting worme, to dust must turn, and worse but for new birth."

But in truth the service of Clio can hardly be profitably mixed with the meditation of other muses, and Johnson's book, in spite of his "meeters" and his excellent intentions, is not a historical source of the first quality. For while he gives much valuable information, especially as to the successive planting of new towns and churches in Massachusetts, he is not seldom inaccurate.

Such were the four historians, and such was the historiography of our first colonial period. Of other writers, whose works were not of purely historical import, or who attained not unto the first four, it is not my purpose to speak. Yet one of these works, Hubbard's "Narrative of the Indian War," a book marked by much vividness of narration, was in its own time esteemed of such importance that, for the perusing and approving it, we are told, "three honorable Magistrates were deputed by the Governor and Council of the Massachusetts Colony (one of whom was a Major-General, and the other two were afterwards Governors)." The whirligig of time brings its revenges. In our day, major-generals and governors, and even presidential candidates, have taken to the writing of history, and the historical scholar has the opportunity of reviewing them.

II.

THE EIGHTEENTH CENTURY.

ACCORDING to the arrangements of chronology, the seventeenth century ended with the year 1700. According to the real facts of history, the period that we always think of as the seventeenth century ended at least a dozen years earlier, and the real eighteenth century then began. In other words, though there was no violent break, yet with the fall of the House of Stuart and the formation of the Grand Alliance a new page in the history of western Europe was turned. The age of Richelieu, of Strafford, of Cromwell, and of Milton had ended; the age of Walpole, of Dubois and Fleury, of Pope and Voltaire, had already begun. A century of prose, of criticism, of wit, and of finish set in. The very wars that have been alluded to are typical of the change. The conflicts in which the preceding generations had been engaged — the Thirty Years' War, the civil wars in England and in France — were conflicts for great religious or constitutional principles. The war which opened with the formation of the Grand Alliance and the expulsion of James II. was more like the wars of the succeeding period, — wars not wholly dynastic, indeed, but of a dryly political character, and waged rather with gallantry than with lofty enthusiasm. Politics, at any rate in England, where alone politics was a popular concern, subsided into a condition unenthusiastic, inanimate, and humdrum. Material prosperity was rapidly increasing, and the world, tired of the age of conflict, became devoted to the pursuit of wealth. Society settled down into that prosaic and secular temper, that engrossment with the material elements of life, that absence of high ideals, to which of late we have been giving the name Philistinism. Political life consisted of little but selfish personal conflicts, between statesmen who laughed good-naturedly at the mention of patriotism or public virtue. The church was lifeless. The world was its own god, and Sir Robert Walpole was its prophet.

The independence of Europe which America has enjoyed since the War of 1812, and has more distinctly felt since the close of the Civil War, inclines us sometimes to speak and think of our earlier history as if an equal degree of independence prevailed in those times. The history of America is written as a separate story, as the story of something quite isolated. In reality, the same waves of thought and feeling generally agitated both, though they sometimes reached the American shores a little later. Fashions in these matters were as naturally followed in the colonies as fashions in dress or in social usages are followed in colonies everywhere. So it happened that the age of Walpole was marked by much the same phenomena on this side of the water as in England. No period in our history was so dull. Political enthusiasm, whether it were enthusiasm for liberty or enthusiasm for loyalty, declined, and gave place to an unheroic apathy. Religious zeal declined not less. Even controversial life in the church was concerned with matters less vital than heretofore; while as to controversies in matters of state, they centred almost universally about interests of a petty and personal and selfish sort, so that history finds little better to record than the quarrels of the royal governors with the colonial assemblies. The country was growing rich and prosperous, and as it sought wealth and prosperity more and more, the intensity which had marked the preceding period rapidly relaxed. The generation grew broader and more tolerant, indeed, but it at the same time grew more worldly and more commonplace in its aims and thoughts.

The incoming of this age of prose had, I am persuaded, more unhappy results in New England than in Virginia, or in the Southern and Middle colonies generally. Its easier tone was better suited to the life and manners that had grown up in those milder and softer climates. The alteration from the seventeenth century was less marked and less demoralizing. But in Massachusetts the candid inquirer is forced to admit a deterioration for which the gain in liberality was hardly a compensation. Few things in our history are more pathetic than the grief of the uncompromising elders when the Massachusetts charter was taken away and the Puritan theocracy fell. But the succeeding generation grew accustomed to the change, and submitted themselves willingly unto Cæsar. The great experiment, the object of so much prayer and solicitude and ceaseless effort, had failed. The strenuousness which had arisen from high aims and devotion to a great and religious task in part gave way, in part became diverted into pettier channels. The elder Puritans had shown harshness and austerity, but mixed with these were elements of grandeur. In the eighteenth century there is much of the same harshness and rigor, but the diary of Judge Sewall, the New England Pepys, shows us minds painfully exercised about small things, — about periwigs and surplices and the observance of Christmas.

Sewall does not properly fall within the scope of these papers. In his solemn yet amusing way, he furnishes us with valuable historical material, indeed, but not with a professed historical composition. But much the same character is borne by the most prominent historian of the age, that redoubtable New England Boanerges, the Reverend Doctor Cotton Mather, the "literary behemoth" of our colonial era, as Professor Tyler has called him; author of no less than four hundred and fifty-two published writings, and especially of the "Magnalia Christi Americana; or, The Ecclesiastical History of New England, from Its First Planting in the Year 1620, unto the Year of our Lord,

1698." This miracle of learning and piety and factious ambition and pedantry and conceit was born to every advantage which could attend a New England historian of the colonial period. He was the grandson of two of the chief lights of the pulpit in the days of the settlement, the Rev. John Cotton and the Rev. Richard Mather. His father, Dr. Increase Mather, was minister of a large parish in Boston, president of Harvard College, himself author of ninety-two writings, and for many years the most influential as well as the most learned man in New England. Great things were expected of one who began life under such auspices, — *non sine dis animosus infans*. Cotton Mather early began to satisfy these expectations. He was graduated from Harvard College at an age younger than that of any bachelors save two in its whole history, and three years later took the master's degree, sustaining in public disputation the thesis that the Hebrew points are of divine origin. His early piety was not less conspicuous. "When he began to speak almost," says his son and biographer, "he began to *pray*, and practiced this Duty constantly while he was a School-Boy; and, altho' he used no *Forms* in Secret, he composed some for his School-Fellows & obliged them to pray. Before he could write notes of Sermons *in public* Assemblies, he commonly wrote what he remembred when he came home. He read the *Scriptures* with so much *Ardor* and Assiduity, that *fifteen Chapters* a Day divided into three Exercises, and nothing less, would suffice him. He would moreover reprove his Play-mates for their wicked Words and Practices." At fourteen he began the practice of frequent fasting.

Not many years after his graduation, this pink of youthful priggery was called to be assistant in his father's church, of which he remained a pastor for nearly half a century, for much of that time directing the affairs of the province, like a pope, from the pulpit of the Old North Church. His rich and fruitful activity in public affairs during that period cannot here be described, although important illustrations of his character may be derived from his course in the witchcraft troubles, in which he was extraordinarily active; urging on the courts to more and more prosecutions, stimulating the popular excitement, and making the most violent efforts to prevent the natural reaction. It is with his literary activities and mental characteristics that we are concerned. His son, relating his death-bed conversation, says: "I asked him *what Sentence or Word, what* Πύκνον Ἔπος, *He would have me think on constantly*, for I ever desired to have him before me and hear him speaking to me? He said, 'Remember only that one word *Fructuosus.*'" The advice was highly characteristic. Never was there a mortal of more prodigious industry. In one year he prepared and published fourteen books, preached more than seventy-two public sermons and nearly half as many private ones, kept sixty fasts and twenty-two vigils, besides attending to his other varied duties, for he was most assiduous in pastoral labors. The amount of his work in the study was enormous; that of his work among men was scarcely less so. The 361st of his works, as catalogued by Mr. Sibley, is entitled "Honesta Parsimonia; or, Time Spent as it should be. Proposals, . . . To prevent that Great Folly and Mischief, The Loss of Time." Herein, at least, the learned and painful doctor practiced what he preached. The record of the various ingenious means which he employed in order not to waste any time is an amusing and interesting one. Even his prayers and meditations and thoughts were carefully systematized. The topic and method of his meditations while dressing were prescribed for each morning in the week. There was method observed even in the occasional thoughts with which he strove to have odd moments profitably occupied.

"When the Doctor waked in the *Night*," says his son, "he would impose it as a Law upon Himself ever before he fell asleep again to bring some *Glory of his Saviour* into his Meditations, and have some agreeable *Desire of his Soul* upon it. . . . When he *washed his Hands*, he must think of the *clean Hands*, as well as *pure Heart*, which belong to the Citizens of Zion. And when he did so mean an Action as *paring his Nails*, he tho't how he might *lay aside all Superfluity of Naughtiness*. . . . He was very constant in *Ejaculatory Prayers and Praises*. . . . While he *walked the Streets*, or *sat in a Room* with his Mind otherwise unemployed, he would not lose the Time, but use his *Wit* as well as *Grace* in contriving some suitable *Blessing* for such and such as were before him; and then he would form it into an *Ejaculation* for them. . . . When he *walked the Streets*, he still *blessed* many Persons who never knew it, with *secret Wishes* after this manner for them ; Upon the sight of a tall man, '*Lord, Give that Man high attainments in Christianity.*' A lame Man, '*Lord, Help that Man on moral Accounts to walk uprightly.*' A Negro, '*Lord, Wash that poor Soul ; make him white by the Washing of thy Spirit.*' A Man going by without observing him, '*Lord, I pray Thee, Help that Man to take a due Notice of Christ.*'" The punning habit which is here noticeable crops out in all his writings, and indeed a general habit of verbal jingles and ingenuities which might justify one in applying to himself what he in the " Magnalia " says in praise of Rev. John Wilson, and commending

" His care to guide his *flock* and feed his *lambs*,
By *words, works, prayers, psalms, alms* and *anagrams*."

Enough has been cited to show thoroughly the character of this extraordinary man, — a man of extraordinary piety, no doubt, but also of extraordinary self-consciousness, rising at times into the most amusing vanity. His tireless energy and industry in study went far towards fitting him to be a historian of New England. His family connections and his prominent position gave him additional facilities for such a task. Already, among his multitudinous publications, he had issued a few minor ones of historical content, such as " The Bostonian Ebenezer," " Decennium Luctuosum," " Arma Virosque Cano," and " A Pillar of Gratitude." But about 1693 he formed the design of writing a general church history of New England, a design which the neighboring ministers much encouraged. It was finished in 1697. On January 12, 1698, he records in his diary: " I set apart this day for the exercise of a secret fast before the Lord. One special design of my supplications was to obtain the direction of Heaven about my ' Church History,' the time and way of my sending it into Europe, and the methods of its publication. I think I am assured that my supplications are heard in this matter." After long delays, an opportunity occurred to send it to London ; but still further delays intervened. The book was large, the publishers were cold ; but at length one was found who, not with any expectation of gain, but for the glory of God, undertook its publication. It may be interesting to note the mode in which the historian manifested his concern for his precious work, — a mode perhaps not often observed by the historians of our day. In his diary, under date of April 4, 1702, occurs the following entry : —

"I was in much distress upon my spirit concerning my 'Church History,' and some other elaborate composures, that I have sent into London ; about the progress towards the publication whereof the Lord still keeps me in the dark. To have those composures, with all my labors and all my prayers about them, lost, would be a terrible trial to me. But I thought it my duty to prepare for such a trial. Wherefore I set apart a vigil this night peculiarly for that service. Accordingly, in the dead of the night, I first sang some agreeable psalms ; and then, casting myself prostrate in the dust, on my studyfloor, before the Lord, I confessed unto him the sins for which he might justly reject me and all my services ; and I promised unto him, that if He would reject those particular services, which I have been laboring to do for His name, in my 'Church History,' and some of the composures now in England, though my calamity therein would be very sensible, yet I would with His help submit patiently unto His holy will therein ; and I would not be discouraged thereby at all from further endeavors to serve my Lord Jesus Christ, but I would love him still, and seek him still, and serve him still, and never be weary of doing so,.but essay to serve him in other ways, if he would not accept of these. Thus did I resign unto the Lord ; who thereupon answered me, that He was my Father, and that He took delight in me, and that He would smile upon my endeavors to serve Him, and that my 'Church History' should be accepted and prospered."

Mather's solicitude for his books, it ought to be said, should not be regarded as arising solely from vanity. The desire to do good by them seems to have been ever present with him. From both motives, he used the utmost care and ingenuity and diligence in disseminating copies of them in all directions, more especially throughout New England, as soon as he received them from the press of Boston or of London. The arrival of the first copy of the " Magnalia " is thus chronicled by him, October 30, 1702 : —

"Yesterday I first saw my 'Church History' since the publication of it. A gentleman arrived here from Newcastle in England, that had bought it there. Wherefore I set apart this day for solemn *thanksgiving* unto God for his watchful and gracious providence over that work, and for the harvest of so many prayers and cares and tears and resignations as I had employed upon it. My religious friend, Mr. Bromfield, who had been singularly helpful to the publication of that great book (of twenty shillings price at London), came to me at the close of the day, to join with me in some of my praises to God."

The offspring of all these " prayers and cares and tears and resignations " is indeed a large book, distended by abundant divagations and moralizings and quotations, and even the insertion, in extended reprint, of essays already published. There is little consistency or method in the mode of presentation. It is the outpouring of a full mind working at great speed. The general scheme is plain enough, but it is such as to involve much repetition and looseness of arrangement. The first of the seven books of which the " Magnalia " consists gives a somewhat desultory history, not only ecclesiastical but civil, of the colonies of New England. As an

appendix to this book is reprinted "The
Bostonian Ebenezer." The second book is
entitled "Ecclesiarum Clypei," and contains
the lives of the governors that were as shields
unto the churches of New England. To
each of the more important ones is conse-
crated a separate chapter, under some such
quaint title as "Nehemias Americanus, the
Life of John Winthrop, Esq., Governour of
the Massachuset Colony." The third book
gives, in forty-three chapters, the lives of
the principal New England divines. The
first part, entitled "Johannes in Eremo"
(John in the wilderness), commemorates four
of the most prominent, grouped together,
for no other reason, apparently, than that
they all bore the name John, — John Cotton, John Norton, John Wilson, and John
Davenport. In the second part (quaintly
entitled "Sepher Jereim, i. e. Liber Deum
Timentium; or, Dead Abels yet speaking
and spoken of"), in the third part, and in
the fourth, other clerical worthies are commemorated who were of less consequence, or
who did not have the name of John. The
fourth book is devoted to the history of
Harvard College, and the biographies of its
more eminent graduates; the fifth, to the

acts and monuments of the New England church. The sixth book, perhaps the most curious of all, is called "Thaumaturgus, . . . *i. e.* Liber Memorabilium, . . . wherein very many illustrious discoveries and demonstrations of Divine Providence in remarkable Mercies and Judgments on many particular persons among the people of New England, are observed, collected and related." One chapter, headed "Christus super Aquas," is given to remarkable deliverances by sea; another, "Ceraunius or Brontologia Sacra," to providences connected with thunder and lightning. Still another has as an appendix a history of criminals executed for capital crimes, with their dying speeches. But the most remarkable of all is that bearing the formidable title "Thaumatographia Pneumatica," and "relating the wonders of the invisible world in preternatural occurrences." "There has been," he says, "too much cause to observe, that the christians who were driven into the *American Desart*, which is now call'd *New England*, have to their sorrow seen *Azazel* [Satan] dwelling and raging there in very tragical instances. The devils have doubtless felt a more than ordinary vexation, from the arrival of those christians with their sacred exercises of christianity in this wilderness: But the sovereignty of heaven has permitted them still to remain in the wilderness, for our vexation, as well as their own." And so he proceeds to a detailed narration of fourteen selected cases of witchcraft, forming a chapter of most curious reading, and a monument of his own ingenuity and credulity. Finally, the " Magnalia " closes with a book called " Ecclesiarum Prœlia, or, A Book of the Wars of the Lord." It is, however, mainly concerned with the conflicts of the colonial authorities against heretics; but at the end it includes a reprint of the two small books, " Arma Virosque Cano" and " Decennium Luctuosum," giving an account of the Indian wars.

Such was the composition of this famous work. Its style was not less peculiar. Prince, indeed, in his funeral sermon upon Mather, confesses that " in his Style indeed He was something singular, and not so agreable to the Gust of the Age." He was probably the most learned man, and certainly had the largest library, in colonial America. The treasures of these intellectual resources were lavished upon his work, until its tissue was heavy and stiff with the jewels of pedantic quotation. It is a very easy matter to appear erudite, and doubtless Mather knew the imposing trick of jauntily alluding to recondite authors, and ignoring their unfamiliarity to writer as well as reader. But with all deductions, he was really very learned. The jewels were genuine enough; the fault was that the fabric was overloaded with them. Some indeed have breathed a suspicion that they were out of all proportion to the value of the ground-stuff. An eminent but crotchety historical scholar of the last generation used systematically to refuse to believe any unsupported statement of Mather. This, however, is unjust. He is often inaccurate, but he has conveyed to us a great amount of information not elsewhere attainable. The criticisms upon his historical style may best be explained by showing a bit of it. With some difficulty, I select a passage not cumbered with Greek and Latin quotations. It is the beginning of the chapter called " Venisti tandem ? or discoveries of America : " —

"It is the opinion of some, though 't is *but* an *opinion*, and *but* of *some* learned men, that when the sacred oracles of heaven assure us, *the things under the earth* are some of those, *whose knees are to bow in the name of Jesus,* by those *things* are meant the inhabitants of *America,* who are Antipodes to those of the other *hemisphere.* I would not quote any words of *Lactantius,* though there are some to countenance this interpretation, because of their being so *ungeographical.* ... I can contentedly allow that *America* (which as the learned *Nicolas Fuller* observes, might more justly be called *Columbina*) was altogether unknown to the *penmen* of the Holy Scriptures, and in the *ages* when the scriptures were penned. I can allow, that those parts of the earth, which do not include *America,* are in the inspired writings of *Luke,* and of *Paul,* stiled, *all the world.* I can allow, that the opinion of *Torniellus,* and of *Pagius,* about the apostles preaching the gospel in *America,* has been sufficiently refuted by *Basnagius.* But I am out of the reach of Pope *Zachary's* excommunication. I can assert the existence of the *American Antipodes;* and I can report unto the *European* churches great occurrences among these *Americans.*"

Even if the Americans were antipodes of Europeans in a geographical sense, which is hardly literally true, they were far from being so in respect to mental development. One of the most interesting facts about Mather as a literary phenomenon is that he is our chief American example of a remarkable historical school then dominant in every part of Europe, and shows America participating in the life and evolution of European thought. The sixteenth century and the early seventeenth had been an age of great historians who were also great men. Prominent statesmen and soldiers wrote brilliant accounts of events in which they had borne an active part. Something of this characteristic belongs, as we have seen in the previous chapter, to the American historical writers of that time. The period from 1650 to 1750, on the other hand, was in Europe distinctively an age of erudition. Excellence in historical narrative declined, but enormous labors of investigation, criticism, and publication were carried through. It was the age of Bollandists and Benedictines, of Mabillon and Muratori and Rymer. In every country giants of erudition arose, and vast additions were made to the sum of historical knowledge. Obviously, Cotton Mather was nowise the equal of these Anakim. But he is their American analogue, and he, and Thomas Prince, and the Rev. William Stith, of Virginia, show us that already the English colonies so far shared the life of the world that even the movements of European scholarship found their counterpart on these shores.

But there was, at any rate, one American historian who was not thus mentally annexed to Europe, but retained an original spirit, racy of the Virginian soil. It has already been remarked that the incoming of the age of Walpole had less undesirable effects in Virginia than in New England. Something must be attributed to the happier influence of the climate; something, to origin from Englishmen whose traditions were not Puritan. But whatever were the causes, the tone of Virginia life and thought in the earlier part of the eighteenth century was an exceedingly attractive one. The tone of Virginia life, I ought perhaps rather to say; for of its thought we really know little. But its life, at any rate, was marked by an openness, a freshness, a geniality, strikingly contrasting with the narrow strenuousness which the decline of Puritan fervor had left behind it in contemporary Massachusetts. The Virginian planters were not less worldly and unheroic, not less the children of the eighteenth century. But their engrossment with the world took the turn of a hearty delight in it, so fresh and spontaneous and agreeable as half redeemed its Philistinism. Of this life, easy-going and commonplace and sterile of intellectual achievement, yet pleasing and natural, we fortunately have an admirable exponent in Robert Beverley. Perhaps it is rather as such an exponent than as a historian that Beverley is valuable to us; for, excellent as his historical narration is, it occupies but little more than a third of the not very large book which, in 1705, he published under the title " The History of Virginia." The rest is descriptive of the natural productions of the country, of the Indians and their civilization, and of the present state of the colony and the nature of its government. It is this last portion, apparently, out of which the volume grew. In his youth, Beverley's father was clerk of the House of Burgesses; he thus became familiar with the public records and public business of the colony, and for his own information gathered many notes regarding its administration. These notes lay unused until the year 1703, when, after the fashion of the wealthy planters of that day, he went to London upon business. Soon after his arrival, his bookseller told him that a general account of all Her Majesty's plantations in America was being prepared for printing, and requested him to look over that part of it relating to Virginia and Carolina. The book was Oldmixon's "British Empire in America." Half a dozen sheets of the manuscript of it were brought to Mr. Beverley. What followed may as well be related in the colonial proprietor's own words as in any paraphrase of them: —

"I very innocently (when I began to read) placed Pen and Paper by me, and made my Observations upon the first Page, but found it in the Sequel so very faulty, and an Abridgment only of some Accounts that had been printed 60 or 70 years ago; in which also he had chosen the most strange and untrue Parts, and left out the more sincere and faithful, so that I laid aside all Thoughts of farther Observations, and gave it only a Reading; and my Bookseller for Answer, that the Account was too faulty and too imperfect to be mended: Withal telling him, that seeing I had in my junior Days taken some Notes of the Government, which I then had with me in England, I would make him an Account of my own Country, if I could find Time, while I staid in London. And this I should rather undertake in Justice to so fine a Country; because it has been so misrepresented to the common People of England, as to make them believe, that the Servants in Virginia are made to draw in Cart and Plow, as Horses and Oxen do in England, and that the Country turns all People black, who go to live there, with other such prodigious Phantasms. Accordingly before I left London, I gave him a short History of the Country, from the first Settlement, with an Account of its then State; but I would not let him mingle it with Oldmixon's other Account of the Plantations, because I took them to be all of a Piece with those I had seen of Virginia and Carolina, but desired mine to be printed by itself."

It is no wonder that Beverley took this course, in view of some of the errors he signalizes in that book. For instance, in one passage Oldmixon said, "When Indians at the Head of the Bay [*i. e.* Chesapeake Bay] travelled to New York, they past, going and coming, by the frontiers of Virginia and traded with the Virginians," etc. Here we have, early exemplified, that originality of view respecting American geography on the part of Englishmen which was until recent times the source of so much vexation to American bosoms, and which, now that we have become less sensitive, proves so perennially amusing.

The paragraph which I have quoted to show the genesis of Beverley's book will also serve to exhibit the merits of his style. It is simple, clear, and direct, far removed from the curious involution and cumbersome pedantry of Cotton Mather's; it never smacks of the lamp. The author was a plain Virginia gentleman, who had read some books, not too many, perhaps, but did not think it necessary to mention them all, nor to quote them with a frequency inversely proportioned to the familiarity of the language in which they were written. A French traveler of the period has left us an interesting picture of the home and the simple rural life of Beverley, whom he happened to visit upon business. It is too long to be here quoted;

but the characteristics which it brings to light are most attractive and Arcadian. Again and again in Beverley's book his strong love of nature crops out, and some of his descriptions are truly delightful. This, however, is in the second, third, and fourth parts of the book. As to the first or historical portion, it is too brief to convey to us a very great body of information on Virginian history; but the sprightliness and ease of the style prevent its ever seeming dry. For the latter years of the seventeenth century, the years just before it was written, its volume becomes greater, and it gives some interesting information on details of public affairs, such as might easily come to the writer not only from his own experience, but from his family connections, for he was brother-in-law at once to President John Robinson and to Colonel Byrd of Westover.

Leaving aside such plain and business-like accounts as that of Beverley, the histories hitherto written in America had mostly been written either for the glory of God, or for the glory of the writer, as in the case of Captain John Smith, or for the glory of both in curious mixture, as in the case of Cotton Mather. It remained for some one to prepare the soil for the growth of American historical scholarship by beginning to write history without didactic or personal tendency, and in a truly scientific spirit. It may fairly be said that the wealth and leisure of the torpid and money-getting age which has been described were necessary prerequisites. The traditional view is that scholarship and poverty are twin sisters. In reality, however it may be of scholarship generally, the thorough pursuit of history requires so much laborious research, and therefore so much leisure on the part of some one, that for its successful conduct it has generally been necessary that, if not the individual, at any rate the age, should be rich. At all events, with the increase of wealth a hundred and fifty years ago, there did appear our first historical scholars, one in Virginia, one in Massachusetts. There was a curious parallelism, not only in their purposes and methods, but also in the unfortunate immediate fate of their books.

The two scholars alluded to are the Rev. Thomas Prince, minister of the Old South Church in Boston, and the Rev. William Stith, president of William and Mary College in Virginia. The elder of the two was the Boston clergyman, a man of high and amiable character, who from his boyhood had possessed an eager interest in whatever bore upon the history of New England. Appreciating more highly than those who had preceded him the need of scholarly thoroughness and the value of original authorities, he spent years in making a search, as exhaustive as he could, for printed and manuscript materials. Thus he formed that invaluable New England Library which has been already more than once referred to, and of which a considerable portion, surviving to our times, forms the priceless Prince Collection in the Boston Public Library. Of books, pamphlets, and printed papers he had accumulated, he tells us, about a thousand; he had also gathered together a multitude of manuscripts left by the early settlers, documents, copies, and letters, to the number of several hundred.

With these copious materials, Prince at length, though with diffidence, began the composition of a Chronological History of New England. His modest aim did not extend to the preparation of a historical composition in the fullest sense; he proposed merely to write a chronology, but with every sort of care to secure the most minute accuracy. He proposed to include "remarkable providences," the deaths of prominent men, brief notices of transactions of the government, elections, grants and settlement of towns, the formation of churches, the ordination and removal of ministers, the erection of important buildings, remarkable laws, executions, wars, battles, — in short, all the events of the earlier history of those colonies in which his contemporaries might feel an interest. In the long introductory portion he notes down, in true annalistic fashion, the principal events in the history of the world from its creation down to the settlement of New England. This, he confesses, gave him a vast amount of trouble; and we must regret that he spent so much time in perfecting it, for the result was that the New England Chronology never got beyond the year 1633. Indeed, the first volume, published in 1736, carried the narrative no farther than to the autumn of 1630. Here the publication rested until eighteen or nineteen years later, when the author, then an old man, began the publishing of volume second by the issue of sixpenny numbers, of thirty-two pages each. Only three such numbers, it is supposed, were ever issued; and of these three no one now possesses a perfect set. The truth seems to be, that there was not at that time an adequate public demand for a history so minute as Prince provided.

It will be evident from the plan of his work that it does not lend itself readily to interesting quotation. But it is the first of our histories, not itself an original source, which is of value as a contribution to historical science rather than to historical literature; and it is to this that it owes its great importance. Prince and his Virginian contemporary are the progenitors of modern American historiography. The wide sweep of the search after materials, the patience and industry in investigation, the minute accuracy and fidelity which characterize the best of the moderns, are all to be found in Prince, and to be found in a high degree. "It is Exactness I aim at," he says, "and would not have the least mistake, if possible, pass to the world. If I have unhappily fallen into any, it is through inadvertency only." The spirit of the work, it will be seen, was that of the Benedictines of St. Maur; and the execution seems to have been as scholarly as the intention.

Among the points of resemblance between Prince and Stith, their ill-success in publication is one of the most remarkable, and in truth not at all creditable to our forefathers. There is something highly amusing in the tone of annoyance with which Stith remarks the indifference of his contemporaries to his labors. After speaking of his intention to have included many more interesting documents, he says: " But I perceive, to my no small Surprise and Mortification, that some of my Countrymen (and those too, Persons of high Fortune and Distinction) seemed to be much alarmed, and to grudge, that a complete History of their own Country would run to more than one Volume, and cost them above half a Pistole. I was, therefore, obliged to restrain my Hand, . . . for fear of enhancing the Price, to the immense Charge and irreparable Damage of such generous and publick-spirited Gentlemen." This, we may suppose, was the reason why the work was never carried beyond the year 1624. If it had been carried down, on the same scale, to the year of publication, 1747, it would have made an eight-volume history of the colony of Virginia, a work of such bulk that even " Persons of High Fortune and Distinction" in Virginia might be excused for hesitating to support it.

Yet these persons might have done well to sustain him, for his "History of the First Discovery and Settlement of Virginia" is an excellent piece of work, — pleasing in style, accurate, and fair. That it is too prolix, however, is a thing that cannot be denied; and this is the more to be blamed because the proportions between the different parts show us clearly that the author was dominated by his materials, rather than master of them, and that he relates much of his story at great length simply because it is in his power to do so. Thus, out of the seventeen years which he treats, he devotes three fourths of his space to the first three years and the last five, evidently because materials were most abundant for these. For the years 1607–1609 he could draw on the most detailed portion of Captain John Smith's narrative, — a source the complete trustworthiness of which he seems in general not at all to doubt, though disposed to make considerable allowances for personal pique and party spirit in regard to Smith's expressions concerning the Virginia Company. "Not," he says, "that I question Captain

Smith's Integrity; for I take him to have been a very honest Man, and a strenuous Lover of Truth."

When this esteemed guide leaves him, the ex-president of William and Mary falls back upon the papers in the Capitol at Williamsburg, and the collection of documents made, for historical purposes, by his late uncle, Sir John Randolph. With the year 1619, however, his narrative widens into a very copious account, which is derived, in a far greater degree than has been generally supposed hitherto, from one of the sources which he mentions. The mode in which he refers to it is as follows: "But I must confess myself most indebted, in this Part of my History, to a very full and fair Manuscript of the London Company's Records, which was communicated to me by the late worthy President of our Council, the Honorable William Byrd, Esq." The records so described have a curious history, and one which, it may be remarked parenthetically, authors have almost invariably related incorrectly. In 1624 King James I. seized the papers of the company and dissolved it. Shortly before this, in anticipation of such a seizure, certain officers of the company had secretly caused to be prepared an attested copy of the records of its proceedings during the last five years, to serve as evidence for their justification in case of prosecution. The copy, when completed, was entrusted to the president of the company, Shakespeare's friend, the Earl of Southampton. On the death of his son, the Lord High Treasurer Southampton, in 1667, the two volumes of the copy were bought of his executors, for sixty guineas, by Captain William Byrd, of Virginia, and for more than a century formed a part of the extensive library of the Byrd family at Westover. These are the two volumes of which Stith made use, and he appears to have used them very freely. All subsequent historians have referred to them, but to all appearances they have not really used them. It would take too long to relate how most of them passed into the possession of Thomas Jefferson, and then into that of Congress. In the Library of Congress these primary sources for the history of our first colony have now been buried for sixty years, and all efforts to make them public have hitherto failed before the apathy of Congress and the difficulties presented by its cumbrous machinery. Extracts from a copy have lately been printed.

The fifth work to be mentioned, the best of all, was written by a man of conspicuous station, — lieutenant-governor, chief justice, and finally governor of Massachusetts, — and was bodily associated with a striking event in our Revolutionary history. The book referred to is the history of the colony and province of Massachusetts by Thomas Hutchinson, the famous Tory governor. The scene alluded to was in the time of the Stamp Act troubles, when already the first volume of the history had appeared. A Boston mob, of the sort which in our school-days we are taught to venerate as gatherings of liberty-loving patriots engaged in resisting oppression, attacked the lieutenant-governor's house. The fact was that he had disapproved of the Stamp Act policy, and had opposed it by every legal means. But liberty-loving patriots engaged in resistance to oppression cannot be expected to give attention to defenses so subtle. They broke in the doors and windows, demolished all the furniture in the house, and destroyed or scattered all the books and papers of the occupant. A clerical neighbor made efforts to save these last, and nearly all of the invaluable manuscript of the second volume of the history was thus preserved. Although it had lain in the street, scattered abroad several hours in the rain, yet so much of it was legible that the author was able to supply the rest, and to transcribe it. In spite of the loss of materials, the second volume was published nine years later. " I pray God," says the writer in his preface, after speaking of the riot, " to forgive the actors in and advisers of this most savage and inhuman injury, and I hope their posterity will read with pleasure and profit what has so narrowly escaped the outrage of their ancestors." It is well known that in this same year the governor retired to England, from which he never returned. Long afterwards, and years after he had died in exile, his grandson, at the request of the Massachusetts Historical Society, published the third volume of the history. The recent publication of his " Diary and Letters " has made clear, to a generation more disposed to be just to those who were faithful to their king, that Governor Hutchinson was, both in patriotism and in character, fully the equal of his opponents. Of his qualities as a historian there is but one opinion. He was industrious in research, and had access to many materials, especially those collected by Cotton Mather, for Mather's son was his brother-in-law. He wrote with excellent judgment, and in a good though not brilliant style. "His mind," says the late Dr. Deane, "was eminently a judicial one; and candor, moderation, and a desire for truth appear to have guided his pen." Even the third volume, which treats of the period from 1749 to 1774, the period in which he was himself so large a figure in the bitter political contests which led to the Revolution, is written with much fairness. The spirit with which Hutchinson approached the history of the colony and province is shown by a note found among his papers, and written near the end of his life, in which he says: —

"In the course of my education, I found no part of science a more pleasing study than history, and no part of the history of any country more useful than that of its government and laws. The history of Great Britain and its dominions was of all others the most delightful to me, and a thorough knowledge of the nature and constitution of the supreme and of the subordinate governments thereof I considered as what would be peculiarly beneficial to me in the line of life upon which I was entering; and the public employments to which I was early called, and sustained for near thirty years together, gave me many advantages for the acquisition of this knowledge."

Here again, as in the case of Cotton Mather and Prince, we may suggest a parallel with the European movements. Hutchinson's approach to historical study was mainly from the point of view of the student of institutional history. In Europe, by the middle of the eighteenth century, the age of erudition had been succeeded by an age mainly devoted to the study of the development of institutions. The Puritan Hutchinson was in his way a member of the school of Montesquieu, Turgot, and Voltaire, — a disciple, consciously or unconsciously, of the " Essai sur les Mœurs."

III.

FROM THE REVOLUTION TO THE CIVIL WAR.

It is difficult to make any general statement concerning the relation which great national crises bear to the development of literature as a whole, or of historical literature in particular. Sometimes, after a nation has passed through a period of struggle, the same mental energy which has carried it through the conflict bursts forth into great literary activity. Sometimes such a period is followed by a time of silence, as if the national forces had been exhausted in military and political effort. In the case of wars for freedom and independence, however, it is generally the former which happens; for, however great the losses of war, the gain of liberty and of opportunity for free expansion is felt to be far more than a compensation, and the sense of freedom gives a freshness and spontaneity that urge toward literary expression. Thus the French Revolution, unfettering all the forces of the national life, brought on a period of activity in historical production more remarkable than any since the sixteenth century, and one noteworthy in general literary activity. The same is in a very high degree true of the heroic and successful struggle of the Netherlanders for freedom. No period in the history of Dutch literature is more brilliant than that which followed the virtual securing of freedom by the Twelve Years' Truce, — a period made brilliant not only by the work of the best poets of the nation, but also by that of some of its best scholars and historians.

In the United States, no movement so noteworthy resulted from the successful accomplishment of the War for Independence. Not much literature of considerable value, historical or other, appeared during or immediately after the Revolution. One reason, no doubt, was that crudity of life and thought which is inevitable to the colonial state; the country was too young and too immature to make it reasonable to expect a great literature. And yet it is to be remembered that, in the period just preceding, so very creditable a piece of work as Hutchinson's "History of Massachusetts Bay" had appeared, giving promise of good things in literature and history. Nor is it an adequate explanation to adduce the undoubtedly great losses which Tory emigration had brought to the classes most likely to be interested in literary development and to further it.

The truth seems to be that, by great and perhaps premature efforts to secure independence, the States had become exhausted to such a degree that the eventual acquisition of freedom, though hailed with loud rejoicings, could not have, upon a people wearied, discordant, and drained of their resources, the vivifying effect which such achievements are wont to have. If one keeps in mind only the year 1776, he will think of the Revolutionary era as a period of national glory; but if he takes into consideration the year 1786, and such incidents as Shays's Rebellion, he will see that at its close the condition of the thirteen bodies politic was far from sound, even though independence had at length been secured. Even the union of 1789 did not at once bring on a healthier state. It was entered into with reluctance, and it was followed by discord. Alexander Hamilton, the young Federalist Rehoboam, laid upon the necks of an unwilling people the yoke of a national consolidation which their fathers had never borne. Availing himself of the general uneasiness, like the wily Jeroboam, the son of Nebat, his astute opponent, Jefferson, summoning discontented Israel to its tents, erected at ancient Beersheba and newly settled Dan the golden calves of the Virginia and Kentucky Resolutions, and through their worship prolonged the congenial Separatism which had descended to this generation from its predecessors. The Revolutionary and Napoleonic wars in Europe delayed still longer the advent of internal tranquillity.

Nevertheless, the years that intervened between the first and the second war with Great Britain were not wholly barren. Something of literature began to grow up, though the flowers that blossomed in the prim and formal inclosures of the "Monthly Anthology" and the "Portfolio" seem to our eyes but a pale and sickly product. Even for history something was being done. The events of the Revolution, still fresh in remembrance, were commemorated in several histories, of which one, at least, — that written by the Rev. William Gordon, — was of great excellence. Biographies of those who had taken a leading part in its events, such as Chief Justice Marshall's celebrated "Life of Washington," were in several instances written with so much care and information that they are among the most important historical authorities for the story of the War for Independence. Often, indeed, those earlier lives have for the student of to-day much more of the attraction of freshness and originality than the biographies written in our own time; the writers of these latter have frequently so full a sense of the American political history of which their subject forms a part that the individuality of the portrait is impaired by the attention paid to the background.

There was also a third class of historical works, to which, in the first years of the republic, important contributions were made. To our minds, the great glory of that period seems manifestly to be the attainment of national independence and national union. To the man of that day, inhabitant of a particular State, and little accustomed to "think continentally," as the phrase was, the thought that his colony had become an independent and sovereign State was often quite as prominent, and was a source of pride and inspira-

tion to a degree difficult for us to conceive.
So it was that all at once, in several of the
newly fledged States, zealous and sometimes
able hands undertook the task of writing
their histories. Several such works, of various degrees of merit, appeared during the
interval between the two wars. Within two
or three years after the conclusion of peace,
David Ramsay, a doctor in Charleston, and
member of the Continental Congress, published a history of South Carolina during
the Revolutionary War, followed later by a
history of the colony and State from the
beginning, which has enjoyed and deserved
a good reputation. Another ex-member of
Congress, Hugh Williamson, published in
1812 a history of North Carolina. In 1804
came a history of Virginia by an Irish jour-
nalist in that State, John Daly Burk. It
cannot be highly praised. But the success
of a book so extensive (four volumes) shows
that, in that commonwealth and elsewhere,
interest in history had advanced greatly
since the time when poor Stith cut short the
superabundant product of his pen because
of inadequate support from "Persons of
high Fortune and Distinction." A few years
earlier came Robert Proud's valued "His-

tory of Pennsylvania," and Benjamin Trumbull's "History of Connecticut;" while, in Massachusetts, George Minot wrote a continuation of Hutchinson's history; and in Georgia, Edward Langworthy prepared a history of that State, since lost. But the best of them all was the Rev. Jeremy Belknap's "History of New Hampshire," which, though published more than a hundred years ago, has never yet been superseded. Beside his industry and fidelity as an investigator, Belknap had a singularly good style. He also edited and published two volumes of American biography, by various hands, which were of real service to American history.

Belknap's writings, however, are not his only, perhaps not his chief, title to recognition by our generation. Our principal debt to him is for his influence, which seems without doubt to have been the dominant influence, in founding the first of the local historical associations of America, the Massachusetts Historical Society, in January, 1791. This was in some degree the beginning of a new phase in the development of American history, though by means of the same local channels through which, as has been said, the current of American historical work mostly ran during the generation succeeding the Revolution. It was the beginning of organized effort. The local historical societies of the present time in the United States are in many cases far from being what we could wish them to be. Some are lifeless, or, like Pope and Pagan in Bunyan's allegory, are toothlessly mumbling over and over again the same innutritious materials; some, that seem full of activity, direct that activity toward any but the most scientific ends. But in their day they have certainly been of great use, and that in two ways: First, they have heightened and fostered by association the growing interest in American history, so long as that interest was mostly for colonial and local history, and until a wider interest should prevail. The local historical society has been, in Paul's phrase, our schoolmaster to lead us to the general study of American history; the study of that national life which in Belknap's time had hardly begun, and which long remained latent or unattractive to the eye of local patriotism.

In the second place, the historical societies have done good service as collectors and publishers of historical materials. The sets of publications of the Massachusetts Historical Society dating from 1792, and those of the New York Historical Society dating from 1811, are invaluable and indispensable. We smile a little over some of the contents of their early volumes, the remarkable articles and bits of information which our naive great-grandfathers thought worth preserving, but which are to us as the poke bonnets and spinning-wheels of old garrets. But side by side with the topographical descriptions of towns, the copies of epitaphs, the accounts of the northern lights, and the letters from a gentleman recently returned from Niagara, there is a part — and really much the larger part — of the early work of these societies which is still valuable. Not only was it of a more scientific character than most of what had preceded it, but it was of peculiar value as establishing a certain tendency in our historical work; a tendency, namely, to make the publication of materials as much an object of the historical scholar's care as the publication of results. The idea has, to be sure, been slow in taking root. Even at the present day it is but a very small part of the population of the United States that can be induced to believe the publication of dry records and documents, well edited, to be not only as useful as the publication of interesting books of history, but, as a general rule, considerably more useful. But in so far as the salutary notion has permeated the public mind, that happy result has been largely due to the wise efforts of those who, eighty or a hundred years ago, were establishing the first local historical societies. A zeal for the collection and preservation of such materials at once arose, one of the first fruits of which was the "Annals of America," which Dr. Abiel Holmes, father of Dr. Oliver Holmes, published in 1805.

It creates some surprise to observe how little was done in the domain of American historical literature in the period between the end of the first administration of Jefferson, that golden age of the young republic and of the Democratic-Republican party, and the times of the rule of Jackson and the new Democracy. Especially singular, at first sight, is the absence of activity during the period immediately succeeding the War of 1812; for, as has already been observed, such activity commonly ensues upon wars which have had an inspiring effect upon the national consciousness. The War of 1812 was anything but glorious, so far as military events were concerned. But, for all that, the popular consciousness was not mistaken in obtaining from it a powerful stimulus to national feeling. Its great result, unmentioned though it was in the Treaty of Ghent, was the immediate emancipation of the United States from colonial dependence on Europe, and from the colonial ideas which still lingered in their politics, and the securing to them of opportunity for unlimited development, on their own lines, of freedom to live their own life.

How profoundly the national consciousness was affected by the opportunity and the responsibility of working out its own salvation may be seen even in the boastful confidence, the crude elation, the vociferous patriotism, and the national arrogance which were so painfully dominant in the America of fifty or sixty years ago, and to which we are wont to give colloquially the name of "Fourth of July." Undoubtedly, America was inspired by the rapidly opening prospect of a boundless career. If the characteristic historical fruits of such inspiration were absent, or at any rate not present in any abundance, we must look for the explanation in that rapid expansion of the nation's material life which went on between 1815 and 1830, and of which the immense westward emigration of those years is but a single though a most conspicuous sign.

When historical literature did start into new life in the United States, such of it as was concerned with American history showed the influence of this popular impulse; but for a while the time of flowering seemed to have been delayed. Usually, periods in which party politics have become quiescent are favorable to the growth of historical literature; and the age of Monroe, an era of good feeling among the people, though one of extremely bad feeling among the politicians, was such a period. But it should be remembered that the impulse of the new era was more likely to be felt by those who were boys at the time of the War of 1812 than by their elders, and therefore would show its effects in literature at a somewhat later date.

As we approach the consideration of the classical period of American historical literature, we find ourselves confronted with a striking fact of geographical distribution. If we tried to name the ten principal historical writers of that period, we should find that seven or eight of them were Massachusetts men, of old New England families, born in or near Boston, and graduated at Harvard College. How are we to account for this extraordinary localization of our science? Of course there are those general causes which produced the remarkable fertility of New England in good literature at that time, and made Boston for so long a period our literary centre, — the greater prevalence of urban life in New England; the indelible intensities of Puritan blood; the inherited traditions of a capital city continuously literary from its origin, and of our oldest college; the stimulating influence of the recent Unitarian revolt, and the resulting controversies; that leaven of buoyant energy in political and literary thought which infused the world in or about the revolutionary year 1830; and other such general causes. But more special explanations are required, for in the case of other sciences and branches of learning we do not find such a proportion obtaining. The other muses were not thus partial to that one city and region; for instance, if political economy has a muse, she was not. Doubtless, something was due to the presence of libraries. History is perhaps more dependent upon these than any other of the departments of literature or science then studied. Large libraries could be found only in those parts of the country where there were cities, and Boston and Cambridge, side by side, with the libraries of the Boston Athenæum and of Harvard College, and later the Boston Public Library, were of all our cities the best provided in this respect. Here, therefore, it might have been expected that historians would congregate, and it has been so. There is one spot of a few acres in Cambridge upon which three of the most eminent historical scholars of the last generation dwelt, and on which have dwelt three of the most prominent historical writers of our own time.

But there was still another reason why history should spring up and flourish in New England, and that was a political one. Throughout our political history we have had two parties which, under various names, have preserved an essential identity. They are usually described as the party of loose construction and the party of strict construction. This is describing them with reference to their attitude toward the Constitution only. A more penetrating analysis will discover in them the party of political measures and the party of political principles, — a party with a programme and a party with a creed. The Democratic party, during its long history, has been mainly marked by its adherence to a certain definite set of political principles. The average American citizen, in quiet times, has had no other political platform than those principles, and has therefore remained a member of the Democratic party. But from time to time there has arisen, out of this mass of Americans unanimous in adhesion to American political principles, a body of men eventually constituting a great party, united in devotion to some great political measure or set of measures, in effort, that is, to alter or add to our political fabric. The Federalist party arose, with a strong sense of work to be done, made its contribution by cementing the Union more firmly, and subsided into the mass of Democracy. With other purposes, but still with purposes of contribution and of alteration, the Whig party arose, did its work, and dissolved. Still a third time, the desire for measures restricting slavery and consolidating still more firmly the national Union drew together a great party which has left its impress indelibly upon our national institutions. Parties marked by this devotion to given political measures will infallibly be loose-constructionist in their view of the fundamental document, as will any body of men, acting under a given instrument, whose main desire is to get certain specific things done: the party of political principles meanwhile adheres to a strict construction.

Now there must of necessity be a radical difference between these two, and between any two bodies of population in which they are respectively dominant, in regard to their attitude toward history. The abstract principles of political philosophy may be supposed to remain ever the same. To the purely legal view of the strict-constructionist, based on these principles, the fundamental relations of politics remain unchanged. That which was the Constitution in 1789 is the Constitution in 1891; and what it is, is to be found by logical reasoning from political principles. The advocate of a programme of measures, of political change, on the other hand, will be constantly recurring to notions of development. To the practical aims which are foremost in his mind, the study of human experience will be of the most direct service, and he and his will incline to historical ways of thinking and to historical studies. It is not an accident that the founder of the Democratic party, with all his interest in science, in philosophy, and in the theory of politics, was but little addicted to the study of history; while his rival, the first Federalist President, was, of all the statesmen of his time and country, the most learned in that department.

To come, then, to the application. Our explanation of the concentration of historical science in the northeastern corner of our country is, in addition to the general reasons for its literary fertility, that the political predilections of the region were such as made the study of human history natural and congenial there. As New England was the chief seat of the Federalist, the Whig, and the Republican parties, the chosen abode of loose construction, it was natural that it should also be the chosen abode of historical science; for no man can escape sharing the interests which political or economical conditions have made most vivid in those around him. We may be confirmed in our view by observing that, in respect to writings of a purely political or economical character, the superiority of the South in both quantity and quality was no less incontestable. As for Massachusetts in especial, it may be observed that in a State where public spirit has always been so strong,—in other words, in a State where the interests and life of the community have been so highly regarded by individuals,—a deep interest in the life and the progressive development of communities is likely to follow.

But before passing to the consideration of our principal schools of classical historians, it may be well to say a word concerning one who belongs to neither North or South,— Washington Irving. We need not speak of him at great length, for his strictly historical works were few, and his fame was mainly achieved in other walks of literature. Nor did he have a great influence upon the development of historical writing among us, unless in the way of general influence upon American style. In fact, it is quite possible that no one of his mature and sober pieces of writing had as much real effect on the progress of American historiography as the admirable humorous composition with which he began, as far back as 1809,—the "History of New York" by Dietrich Knickerbocker. Aside from its striking success as a literary production, the book had a great effect in awakening interest in the early or Dutch period of New York history. Descendants rushed with sober indignation to the defense of ancestors at whom the genial humorist poked his fun, and very likely the great amount of work which the state government in the next generation did for the historical illustration of the Dutch period, through the researches of Mr. Brodhead in foreign archives, had this unhistorical little book for one of its principal causes. But, on the other hand, he made it permanently difficult for the American public to take a serious view of those early Dutch days. Oloffe the Dreamer and Walter the Doubter, Abraham with the ten breeches and Stuyvesant with the wooden leg, have become too thoroughly domesticated among us to admit of that.

In 1828 appeared the "Life and Voyages of Columbus." The short time in which it was prepared, not more at any rate than two years, shows that it cannot have been a work of original research carried out absolutely after the modern manner. It was in fact based on the documentary publications of Don Martin Fernandez de Navarrete, though with much use of the libraries of Obadiah Rich, then our consul at Madrid, of Navarrete himself, of the Duke of Veragua, and of the Council of the Indies, and of other libraries at Madrid and Seville. The result was an excellent piece of historical work, as well as a literary production which it would be superfluous to praise. At about the same time the author proposed a series of writings on the Arabs in Spain, beginning with some account of Mohammed himself. The fruit of this project, the book entitled "Mahomet and his Successors," made no pretensions to original research, and appeared, as did the "Life of Washington," many years after the period which we have been considering.

The very fact that we pass over books not based on original research shows of itself that the period which we are approaching was one marked by higher ideals of historical scholarship than had prevailed before. When this classical period of American historical writing does arrive, it is found to be marked from the first by two separate tendencies; there are, we may almost say, two schools, distinct throughout the period.

On the one hand, we have the historians who have devoted themselves to picturesque themes lying outside the history of the United States, — men whose traditions and associations have been mainly literary, of whom Prescott, Motley, and Parkman are the types. On the other hand, there are the historians who have interested themselves in American affairs, whose associations and impulses have in many cases been in a great degree political, but who have been more especially the inheritors of those impulses already spoken of as marking the early years of the century. The chief example of this last division is George Bancroft, whose honored life was so exceptionally prolonged that he was enabled to give to one great work the labor of fifty years, an experience unexampled in the annals of historical literature. The first volume of his "History of the United States" was published in 1834; the author's last revision was put forth in 1883; and he died but a few months ago, at the age of ninety, having lived almost as many years as Ranke, and with as severe an industry.

If we speak of the product of his long period of labor in connection with the date of its commencement rather than of its close, it is because the work, from its very beginning, has not ceased to bear some marks of an origin in the year 1834. At that time Mr. Bancroft was thirty-four years old. Graduated early from Harvard, he had next had the privilege of university training in Germany. This was in those days a very unusual opportunity. It is amusing to read of the difficulties which, at the modern Athens itself, George Ticknor encountered in 1813 in preliminary movements toward a course of study at Göttingen. "I was sure," he relates, "that I should like to study at such a university, but it was in vain that I endeavored to get farther knowledge upon the subject. I would gladly have prepared for it by learning the language I should have to use there, but there was no one in Boston who could teach me. . . . Nor was it possible to get books. I borrowed a Meidinger's Grammar, French and German, from my friend Mr. Everett, and sent to New Hampshire, where I knew there was a German Dictionary, and procured it. I also obtained a copy of Goethe's 'Werther,' in German, . . . from amongst Mr. J. Q. Adams's books, deposited by him, on going to Europe, in the Athenæum," etc.

This was in 1813, and it cannot have been much different in 1818, when Bancroft went to Göttingen. The two years spent there seem to have been given to quite general studies. In such studies as were historical, it is not to be thought that in the days before Ranke had appeared, and before any permanent work of Niebuhr had been published, it was possible to find in Germany such inspiration for historical studies as in times more recent, even had the young American yet resolved upon such studies. What could be obtained was a much better knowledge of methods and results than America afforded. Of those historians under whom Bancroft studied, Heeren, Savigny, Schlosser, one cannot in his History find trace of much influence, except that Heeren's interest in the history of colonies and of their reflex action upon the mother country probably bore fruit later. Of method he may have earned much from these teachers; his ideas were derived elsewhere, and mainly, in truth, from the soil from which they sprang. They are the ideas of America in the year 1834. The extraordinary popularity of the early volumes can be accounted for only in view of this fact. For the popularity of the later volumes, it is not necessary to resort to any other explanation than that of the enormous amount of labor and care expended on them, the very unusual facilities in respect to access to archives and masses of correspondence which the author's diplomatic positions afforded him, and the encyclopædic fullness and minuteness of his knowledge of his subject. But for the earlier volumes these explanations fail us. If they surpassed in research and scientific value the average of that time, they were still not highly remarkable in those respects. And yet the tenth edition of the first volume was published within ten years of the date of the original edition. The book at once took rank as the standard history of the United States. Thousands and thousands of copies have since been sold. At Washington, upon the doors of the Senate and House of Representatives, its writer's name has long appeared, almost the sole name of a private person in the brief list of those to whom our legislative bodies have given the privilege of entrance upon their floors.

Whence did this immediate and unbounded popularity and acceptance arise? Mainly, I believe, from the fact that the historian caught, and with sincere and enthusiastic conviction repeated to the American people, the things which they were saying and thinking concerning themselves. One need not imitate the professional scorn of the Pharisee and declare that the people that knoweth not the esoteric law is cursed, and yet may freely hold the opinion that the popularity of a work of national history does not depend on the profundity and skill of its research, nor on the correctness and completeness of its results, nor even on its qualities of arrangement and style, so much as on the acceptableness to the national mind of the general idea which it exhibits in regard to the nation's development. Bancroft's first volume succeeded mainly because it was redolent of the ideas of the new Jacksonian democracy, — its exuberant confidence, its uncritical self-laudation, its optimistic hopes. The Demos heard, as an undercurrent to his narrative, the same music which charmed its ears in the Fourth of July oration; indeed, many of Bancroft's most characteristic ideas are to be found in his own oration pronounced at Northampton on July 4, 1826; and the style was one whose buoyancy of rhetoric was well suited to those sanguine times. It would be but a shallow criticism that should see in all this only the ebullition of national vanity. The uncritical patriotism of those times, as of other times in the course of history, was in some respects admirable, and in many respects useful. But we need not forget that it *was* uncritical. The opening words of the introduction to the book will serve as well as any to exhibit what is meant: —

"The United States of America [it begins] constitute an essential portion of a great political system, embracing all the civilized nations of the earth. [This bears the stamp of Heeren's ideas.] At a period when the force of moral opinion is rapidly increasing, they have the precedence in the practice and the defense of the equal rights of man. The sovereignty of the people is here a conceded axiom, and the laws, established upon that basis, are cherished with faithful patriotism. While the nations of Europe aspire after change, our Constitution engages the fond admiration of the people by which it has been established. . . . Our government, by its organization, is necessarily identified with the interests of the people, and relies exclusively on their attachment for its durability and support. Even the enemies of the state, if there are any among us, have liberty to express their opinions undisturbed, and are safely tolerated where reason is left free to combat their errors. Nor is the Constitution a dead letter, unalterably fixed; it has the capacity for improvement, adopting whatever changes time and the public will may require, and safe from decay, so long as that will retains its energy. . . . Other governments are convulsed by the innovations and reforms of neighboring states; our Constitution, fixed in the affections of the people, from whose choice it has sprung, neutralizes the influence of foreign principles, and fearlessly opens an asylum to the virtuous, the unfortunate, and the oppressed of every nation."

The passage is typical, both as to style and as to doctrine. Its sincerity is so manifest that it is impossible not to admire and be touched by its ardent Americanism, its faith in popular government, in the American Constitution, and in the boundless success of the United States through material progress and the simple arts of peace. But a generation which has grown accustomed to less use of literary as well as other stimulants probably finds its eloquence somewhat turgid, and tempers its enthusiasm with the sadder consciousness of a success less perfect than was anticipated. The same qualities and the same defects are to be found in all the subsequent volumes of the work; up to its completion in 1885, it still continued, as our phrase is, to vote for Jackson. But if there had been, meantime, no change in the fundamental principles, there was a great improvement in the workmanship. It is sufficient evidence of this to point to the rate of production of the individual volumes. The first three volumes appeared in 1834, 1837, and 1840; the next three, after a period of political and diplomatic life, in 1852, 1853, and 1854; the seventh and eighth, at intervals a little greater; the ninth, not until 1866; the tenth, in 1874; the two concluding volumes, as late as 1882.

From 1846 to 1849, the historian was our minister to England, and from 1866 to 1874 he was minister in Germany. The result was the collection of an enormous mass of material from the archives of foreign states, and from the stores of family correspondence. Because of the long duration and the great fame of his researches, similar opportunities, almost unlimited in extent, were at his service in this country. Sometimes his narrative seems too much dominated by the possession of the abundant materials of this class to which his prefaces refer with so conscious a pride. The last volumes are limited in scope, giving a history of little but military and diplomatic movements during the Revolution. Perhaps it is as well. Bancroft's talents for the narration of military and diplomatic history were of a very high order. He had great skill in marshalling large arrays of facts, good judgment, and a lucid and picturesque style. On the other hand, a history of popular movements, of public opinion and of the internal development of the United States, would exhibit at the greatest disadvantage the author's faults, — not only his loud and uncritical Americanism and his rhetorical bias, but the superficiality of his insight into national psychology, his failure to perceive its complexities, his tendency to conventionalize, to compose his American populations of highly virtuous Noah's-ark men. The excursuses in which he attempts this are among the least happy and adequate portions of his work.

An interesting though far from pleasing episode in the history of Bancroft's labors was the chapter of controversies with critics. A slighting remark respecting a predecessor, in the second volume of the history, had drawn upon the historian the wrath of the old president of Harvard College, who soon showed that his Federalist pen had not lost its incisiveness and vigor. For reasons partly personal, partly political, Bancroft was highly unpopular in the literary society of Boston, and not a few attacks followed. The ninth volume of the history, dealing with a great part of the military history of the Revolution, aroused an especially large number of assailants. Descendants of Greene, Reed, Schuyler, and Sullivan, in able pamphlets, attempted to show that the historian had dealt unjustly with their respective ancestors. The historian was so much superior to his critics in knowledge and skill, that in most cases he seemed to come off victorious from the encounter. But the careful reader of this mass of controversial literature will probably feel that a good number of the criticisms made were just, especially as concerned Bancroft's use of quotations, which he sometimes so excises and transposes as strangely to pervert their meaning. He will note, too, the haughtiness and acerbity of temper with which criticisms were received, the slender recognition of fellow-laborers, and, where criticisms had been supported by proof, the grudging and minimized acknowledgment of error. But, in spite of all these defects, the American people owe a great debt to the famous historian who has just departed, after a long lifetime spent in enthusiastic study and inspiring exposition of their history.

A few words should be said concerning some other writers of the period, who gave themselves to the sober field of American history. It would be pleasant to be able to say more than a word of Peter Force, of whose great collection of the " American Archives " Congress published nine volumes and then stopped. To the lasting disgrace of Congress, all subsequent efforts have failed to obtain appropriations for the completion of this monumental work. The work of collection and publication was carried on in more varied ways by President Sparks. In making his large collections in America and Europe, and in editing the " Library of American Biography," the writings of Washington and

Franklin, and the " Diplomatic Correspondence of the Revolution," he performed services of inestimable value to American history. That he at the same time did it no small disservice by his mode of editing, as when he toned down the actual words of Washington into tame correctness, was vigorously charged by Lord Mahon and others. Sparks's letters in answer to Mahon were models of dignified reply to criticism. The view of the controversy which would now be taken is, probably, that President Sparks did not conform to all the best rules of editing as they were then known. It is quite true that he ought not to be judged by the more exacting standards of the present day; yet 1833, when Ranke was already teaching and writing, and the "Monumenta" had begun to be published, was by no means in the dark ages of historical method. But there was much exaggeration in the fault found with Sparks, and due recognition of his invaluable pioneer work will prevent extreme censoriousness as to defects of workmanship. Gentle Washington Irving thus alludes to the fault, when speaking of these letters in the preface of his " Life of Washington : " —

"A careful collation of many of them with the originals [Sparks had to work from the letter-books mostly] convinced me of the general correctness of the collection, . . . and I am happy to bear this testimony to the essential accuracy of one whom I consider among the greatest benefactors to our national literature."

Downright Hildreth alluded to it in terms more direct.

Hildreth's own work came later, — late enough to feel the force of increasing sectional animosities, and to show the effects of them in an unfortunate degree. A man of very decided convictions, and ardently interested in politics, the Whig editor wrote the "History of the United States" with a strong partisan bias. In the first three volumes, bringing the story down to the close of the Revolution, this naturally finds less place, and the lucidity, directness, and accuracy of the writer made his book one of much value, though a little dry to the general reader. But in the last three volumes, treating the history of our national politics down to 1821, its partisanship of the Federalists is so manifest that all its lucidity, directness, and general accuracy cannot wholly redeem it. If for Federalists we substitute Democrats, we shall have to say much the same things of the otherwise excellent "History of the United States" to 1841, which George Tucker of Virginia published just before the outbreak of the Civil War. In 1859 and 1860 appeared the first two volumes of the "History of New England" by John Gorham Palfrey, as good a piece of work as had ever been done among us; but it belongs quite as much to the next period, in which the remaining volumes were published; and it is time to turn to the writers of what I have called another school.

It was something more than a difference of subject that separated the writers already characterized from Prescott and Motley. A difference of attitude underlay the difference in choice of subject. The impulses which actuated the former were founded, sometimes in political but at any rate in national feelings. Those of the latter were rather those of the literary man. It was only after long hesitation and with some regret that Prescott abandoned the plan of devoting himself entirely to the history of literature. He was averse to politics, though the historians of Europe have seldom been more engaged in them than they were in his time. His correspondence and his prefaces show us how much the literary aspect of his work occupied him; truthful and artistic narration was his main aim. Writers of such predilections as these would be likely to turn away from the sober history of their own country, and seek their themes in the more picturesque fields of European history. The choice of subjects which Prescott made gives the plainest evidence of such purposes. Even apart from the brilliant treatment which his genius gave them, and from which it is hard for our minds now to separate them, it is plain that the reign of Ferdinand and Isabella, the conquest of Mexico, the conquest of Peru, the history of Philip the Second, were subjects eminently capable of picturesque treatment.

The reader's interest in the volumes written upon these engaging themes is heightened by the knowledge of the difficulties surmounted in their preparation. Like three other eminent historians, his contemporaries, Augustin Thierry, Karl Szaynocha, and the Marquis Gino Capponi, he was blind, or nearly so. Everett, speaking at the memorial meeting of the Massachusetts

Historical Society just after his death, beautifully applied to him the words of the Greek poet, "Greatly the Muse loved him, and she gave him both good and evil; she deprived him of his eyes, but gave him the gift of sweet song." Only during the composition of the second of his books, "The Conquest of Mexico," was he able to make any considerable use of his eyes. During a part of the ten years given to the preparation of the "History of Ferdinand and Isabella," and of the time spent on the "Conquest of Peru," he could use them for an hour or two each day. During the rest of the time, including the whole period given to the "History of Philip the Second," he was forced to rely entirely upon the eyes of others. In fact, his investigations for the first of his books began by going through seven quarto volumes in Spanish, with a reader who understood not a word of the language. Better assistance was eventually procured, and great amounts of reading were done. The writing machine now preserved in the cabinet of the Massachusetts Historical Society was obtained, and released the patient scholar from the necessity of constant dictation. Fortunately, he possessed ample means for the purchase of books. The consultation of foreign archives in person was, indeed, impracticable. But, through the kindness and exertions of devoted friends, of whom his amiable and winning character had attracted a large number, this obstacle was in a great degree removed, and the successive narratives rest on an increasing amplitude of original and unpublished documents, drawn not only from public and private repositories in Spain, but in the case of Philip the Second from most of the great collections of Western Europe. But, for all this, the writing of these eleven volumes under such disabilities remains a most remarkable achievement, and one which bears strong testimony to the high qualities of Prescott's character.

The books themselves need no factitious interest arising from the knowledge of the circumstances of their production. They are too admirable and too familiar to need praise in respect to interest of narrative, grace of style, or artistic skill in the management and marshaling of the various parts. The unity of design and beauty of detail, the romantic charm and picturesqueness which the author sought, he certainly obtained. Scarcely less praise must be given to the conscientiousness of his research, though it may be doubted whether his critical insight was of the most penetrating sort. Nor was he a profoundly philosophical historian, distinguished for searching analysis. In one of his early private memoranda, he confesses that he hates "hunting up latent, barren antiquities," and though he later, to some extent, conquered this repugnance, the studies which make the analytical and sociological historian were never thoroughly congenial to him. It is mainly the concrete aspects of life that engage his interest, and as a historical painter of these, he was, in the period of the publication of his works, the years from 1837 to 1858, without a rival, save Macaulay and Michelet.

In the preface to the first volume of his "Philip the Second," confessing the difficulty of imparting unity of interest to a narrative which must necessarily embrace topics so various, Prescott had alluded particularly to the subject of the revolt of the Netherlands. He had said that, though but an episode to his own subject, this alone might well form the theme of a separate and extensive work, and had announced that before long such a work might be "expected," to use his own words, "from the pen of our accomplished countryman, Mr. J. Lothrop Motley, who, during the last few years, for the better prosecution of his labors, has established his residence in the neighborhood of the scenes of his narrative." The work thus announced, the famous "Rise of the Dutch Republic," was published in 1856. Accordingly when, in 1859, Prescott died, leaving his "History of Philip the Second" no farther advanced than to the year 1580, the historian who should in a sense continue his work was already in the field. The first of Motley's works carried down to the year 1584 a narrative whose subject, though not the same as that of Prescott's last work, necessarily had much in common with it. For the history of the Dutch revolt against Philip could hardly be written without saying much concerning other aspects or portions of his reign. In the year 1860 appeared the first two, in 1868 the last two, volumes of the "History of the United Netherlands," embracing the years 1584 to 1609. "The Life and Death of John of Barneveld," a work in form biographical, but really continuing the "History of the

Netherlands" for a decade more, appeared in 1874.

Enormous labors in the investigation of archives were performed in the preparation of these books. Motley had the intense zeal of the born investigator, a rare and heroic quality of which the world takes little note in historians. He had likewise in full possession those qualities which engage the reader. No American has ever written a history more brilliant and dramatic. The subject was a noble one. It was full of picturesque incident, of opportunities for glowing description, of thrilling tales of heroism. But it was not simply these that so engaged Motley's interest that, as he afterwards said, he felt as if he *must* write upon it. It was a great national conflict for freedom, and as such was profoundly congenial to one who, above all things, loved liberty. The warm heart and enthusiastic, ardent temper of the historian laid him open to dangers of partiality which, it must be confessed, he was far from wholly escaping. The American public little appreciate the extent to which he was influenced by such feelings. Guizot, in a review article, noted Motley's advocacy, but thought it too appa-

rent to do harm, and excused it as being on
the right side, that of political and religious
liberty. Throughout the volumes on the
"Rise of the Dutch Republic," Motley is a
thorough partisan of William the Silent, —
a sincere and conscientious partisan, to be
sure, but a partisan none the less. Some
may think that it is little harm to exaggerate
the virtues of William the Silent, or to
soften the defects of a character so heroic;
but certainly it is a pity to add one more to
the long chain of English writers who, out
of ancestral prejudice, have dealt hard measure to all Spaniards. Similarly, in his narrative of the great internal contest between
the adherents of Prince Maurice and the
adherents of Oldenbarneveld, the Calvinists
and the Arminians, it must be declared de-
liberately that Motley is a partisan of the
latter, and is distinctly unfair to the former.
It is easy to see the reasons in both cases.
As a lover of liberty, the cause of William
and the Netherlanders, fighting for freedom,
engaged his warm affection. In the later
period, his Unitarian sympathies made it
natural for him to embrace the cause of
the Arminians against the Calvinists. Dr.
Holmes, to be sure, in his memoir of Motley,

defends him from this latter charge. The Dutch historian, Groen van Prinsterer, in his " Maurice et Barneveld," though expressing a warm admiration for Motley, has criticised him as unfair to the Remonstrant cause. With his usual keen scent for Calvinism, the doctor endeavors to show that Mr. Groen van Prinsterer has taken up this position because he is himself a Calvinist. But Mr. Groen van Prinsterer does not stand alone. It should not be forgotten that, if none of the Dutch historical writers were as brilliant as Motley, the nation stood, in historical scholarship, hardly second to any in Europe; five historians could be named every one of whom was probably as learned in the facts as Motley himself. The dispute is, in the end, one for the Dutch to settle, and Dutch opinion is still divided. But so long as the leading opinions are in general more moderate than Motley's, and so long as the Dutch are not " vehemently suspected " of having more of the ardent temper of the advocate than Motley had, we may feel justified in mingling a certain sense of partiality with our strong admiration of his warmth, his brilliancy, and his dramatic force.

IV.

THE PERIOD SINCE 1861.

We were able to make a sharp division between the first period in the history of American historical writing and the second; the first chapter including writers who were themselves of the emigrating generation, while in the second none were included who were separated from the original settlers by a less interval than two generations. Similarly, the second period was plainly separated from the third by the revolutionary war, during the distresses and troubles of which there was little leisure for historical or other composition. The historical literature of the colonial period was confined to a few sporadic writers, not organically connected one with another; it had not acquired momentum enough to carry it in continuous life across that time of difficulty and preoccupying care.

But with the third and fourth periods the case is different. American historical literature had now acquired vitality, and henceforth its development was uninterrupted. If, therefore, we select any chronological point at which to divide this last and most important period, the point chosen will necessarily seem from some points of view an arbitrary one. It is quite true that the civil war formed the starting point for many new tendencies in our historical, as in our general literature. But, on the other hand, much went on as before. In the first place, some of the histories spoken of in the last paper, though begun before the war, were not completed until after it. The first two volumes of Motley's " History of the United Netherlands " had appeared in 1860; the last two were published in 1868; and his " Barneveld," which is virtually a continuation of them, in 1874. Another work, whose publication similarly overlapped the fourth period, was Palfrey's " History of New England," probably the best single large piece of work that has been done in America on any part of our colonial period. After much labor in America and considerable research in England, the first and second volumes had been successively published just before the war broke out. The third did not follow until 1865; the fourth, not until 1875. At the writer's death the history of the New England colonies had been brought down to the year 1740; the fifth volume, recently published, carries it to the outbreak of the Revolution. If Dr. Palfrey was not a man of great insight into popular movements, and was too constant an apologist of the rulers of New England, his book was nevertheless admirable on account of his extensive knowledge of sources, his industry, clearness, accuracy, and skill in narration. Among its many excellences, one which deserves particular notice is the degree of attention which it bestows upon the history of England itself during the Puritan era, and upon the mutual influence of Old England and New England during that period of exceptionally close sympathy and connection. Often the genius of a writer is quite as much displayed by new apportionments of their relative amounts of attention to the different aspects of his subject as in any other way, for thus his insight into the proportions and relations of various factors is practically displayed.

Meanwhile, other historians, not in the field during the preceding period, have continued the traditions of the school which has been described in a previous article under the names of Prescott and Motley. An especially close example of this is the case of John Foster Kirk, who was one of the private secretaries successively employed by Prescott, and who, after Prescott's death, wrote a valuable book upon the "History of Charles the Bold," a contribution in the same general field as that of his master's labors. But the author who has most conspicuously continued the school of picturesque historians is Francis Parkman, the eminent historian of the French dominion in North America.

The subject is one highly attractive to an American historical writer of this school, who wishes at the same time that his studies shall not be too remote from his own age and country. Chivalry and heroism and romantic adventure, the glamour of a foreign civilization and the poetic charm of unfamiliar forms of religion, are all there; but the story has also a close and important relation with the growth of our own nation. Prescott had been able to impart an additional interest to his "History of Ferdinand and Isabella" because of the episode formed by the voyages of Columbus; and perhaps Mot-

ley's history of the struggle of the Dutch
for independence may have had a special
interest for the general reader in a country
of whose history a struggle for independence
is one of the most familiar portions. Prescott, too, had chosen distinctly American
subjects in his " Conquest of Mexico " and
his " Conquest of Peru." But no one of
these had so direct a bearing on our national
history as the story of New France. For
several generations some of the most important English colonies were occasionally men-
aced and always limited by the presence
upon their frontier of a considerable military
power established there by a nation usually
unfriendly. Furthermore, the presence of
this power was one of the chief influences
toward colonial consolidation, and its final
removal was one of the causes which made
possible the revolt from the government of
Great Britain. It is therefore with good
reason that the general title given to the
whole series of Mr. Parkman's narratives is,
" France and England in North America."

The project of a series of so wide a scope
developed gradually in the writer's mind.
Soon after graduation from college he had
gone on several occasions to make more or

less extensive visits to the wild regions of the Northwest. Much of his subsequent historical work shows the effects of the familiarity thus gained with the scenery and men of the wilderness. One of these effects was the choice, for the subject of his first historical production, of the Conspiracy of Pontiac. It was from this work that the writer was led on to the preparation of a series of historical narratives upon the whole course of the French dominion in America, its relations to the English colonies, and its final destruction by the military power of Great Britain. For the history of Pontiac's conspiracy forms a natural sequel to the history of the French and Indian war, and to that of New France generally.

This book completed, therefore, and published in 1851, the author went back to take up at the beginning the history of the French in North America, the great task upon which he has been engaged ever since, and which is now nearly completed. As in the case of Prescott, physical difficulties which might well seem insurmountable opposed. Extreme ill health made it always necessary to confine mental exertion within narrow limits, and more than once stopped it entirely for several years at a time. Weakness of sight seems to have made it always impossible to read or write continuously for much more than five minutes, while once, at least, it has been for a period of three years impossible to endure the light of day, or to read or write to the smallest extent.

But the volumes composed under the pressure of these calamities need no indulgence from the critic. It may almost be said that they need no praise, so widely spread and so permanent has been their fame. The first of the series, though published only twenty-seven years ago, has already long passed its twentieth edition. Others are approaching it. The series has shown a continuous improvement, and especially in thoroughness and fullness of research. It is in this respect, indeed, that American historians have, at the outset of their careers, been least adequately provided. In Germany the class of historical writers and the class of historical professors are so nearly identical that the young student who starts out upon a career of historical authorship has almost always the advantage of having learned his trade under a teacher experienced in it. In other words, with all the opportunity it presents, and the need it has for that genius and insight and maturity which can neither be communicated nor described, there are many things in the more technical portions of the pursuit which by long experience have been reduced to practical rules; and these rules can be learned of a master, if only by imitation. But English and American historical writers have till lately worked so much in isolation that they could have no apprenticeship in the communicable portions of the art. In the highly developed arts of research and of historical criticism, therefore, our historians have started out uninstructed, and have learned these as they went on, with no other teachers than their own mistakes and their constant desire for completeness. There has also been a great improvement in the always brilliant and engaging style of Mr. Parkman, which, with increasing years, has grown more severe in taste.

The first book of the projected series was called "Pioneers of France in the New World." Its first part described in fascinating narrative the history of the Huguenot settlement in Florida, and its extinction by the Spanish; the second took up the story of the permanent beginnings of the French dominion, the settlement of Acadia, and the labors of Champlain and his associates. The next volume, published two years later, continues the story from 1635 to 1652, under the title of "The Jesuits in North America." For this volume especially, the author was able to make great use of his early acquired knowledge of Indian character and civilization; the sublime devotion of the missionaries and their heroic endurance of torture and martyrdom at the hands of the savages confer upon it an additional and most touching interest. The next volume, "La Salle and the Discovery of the Great West," treats of an episode, though an episode whose consequences were at one time likely to be highly important. The volume called "The Old Régime in Canada" is devoted, after the narration of the history of the transitional period 1652-1672, to a description of Canadian government and life, in chapters carefully based on original sources, and of surpassing interest. The ablest of the colonial governors and the history down to 1701 are treated in the volume called "Count Frontenac and New France under Louis XIV." The intermediate period to 1748 having been left for the time being, Mr.

Parkman has given us the conclusion in "Montcalm and Wolfe," two volumes, the best in the series, on that American portion of the seven years' war which we are wont to call the French and Indian war.

It will be seen how wide is the range of interest covered by these volumes. They are not simply a history of a great attempt to create, under the forms of absolute monarchy, feudalism, and Catholicism, a centralized and military power. Nor are they simply a history of the efforts of that power to overbalance and check the system of free, Protestant and English colonies, unorganized and discordant indeed, but strong with the strength of popular institutions, of love of freedom, and of habits of individual initiative. This alone would be sufficient to make the tale bright and commanding. But we have also the adventures of explorers and traders, the achievements of missionaries, the heroism of martyrs, the wild life of the Indian tribes, the scenery of the forest, the events of war, the brilliant picture of French aristocracy transferred, for purposes of war or government or devotion, to the wilds of America; and it cannot be said that the writer has proved unequal to the adequate treatment of a single one of these so varied elements of interest.

I have devoted much space to Mr. Parkman as being, next after one or two who survived from the preceding period, the most conspicuous figure in the American historiography of the last twenty-five years, the only historian who can fairly be called classical. No one can predict the advent of genius, but it appears not very likely that the roll of the classical historians will be much increased in the immediate future, or that the next generation will in this respect abound in eminent names. Amiel says: —

"The era of mediocrity in all things is commencing. Equality begets uniformity, and we divest ourselves of the bad by sacrificing the eminent, the remarkable, the extraordinary."

Such, at any rate, is likely to be the case with our historical writing for a long time. Nor is it in the main to be regretted. If there is not produced among us any work of supereminent genius, there will surely be a large amount of good second-class work done; that is, of work of the second class in respect to purely literary qualities. Now it is the spread of thoroughly good second-class work

— second-class in this sense — that our science most needs at present; for it sorely needs that improvement in technical process, that superior finish of workmanship, which a large number of works of talent can do more to foster than a few works of literary genius. If, therefore, that leveled Americanism toward which M. Renan tells us that the world is now progressing is, in the matter of historical work, to take among us the form which we have been supposing, we need not lament. We may even hope that out of improved scholarship may grow in time a superior profundity of thought; for in truth profundity of thought has not been among the merits of any of our most distinguished historians. We may do well to remember that, in the historical literature of Europe, when the Anakim of the sixteenth century were replaced by the mousing but erudite Bollandists and Benedictines of the seventeenth and the first half of the eighteenth, it was only that the way might be prepared, by patient and scholarly accumulation of materials, for the advent of a school of historians more philosophical and profound than any that had preceded.

But the series of American historians to

which Motley and Parkman belong was not characterized solely by the pursuit, in general, of literary ends. Another distinguishing mark was its devotion to European rather than to American history. In our time the devotees of European history are not numerous in the United States (indeed, if one can judge from the contents of our magazines, European history is hardly at all a matter of interest to most Americans); and such devotees as there are have not all inherited the literary traditions. A few scholars have done excellent work in church history, for the cultivation of which a special society has been formed. Most eminent among these is the learned layman whose "History of the Inquisition" has reflected so much honor upon American scholarship. Almost no American has done anything worth while in the study of ancient history. This is a striking fact, when one thinks of it. The history of Rome, especially, offers, one would think, much that should interest Americans. There is even a similarity of national character; the faces upon Roman busts are such as one might see any day in the streets of New York or Philadelphia. When one considers how large a place the study of the classics has long had in American education, one cannot help feeling that such lack of interest in the history of the classical nations indicates that the instruction has not been sufficiently vital. On the other hand, a very respectable number of scholars are at work in lines of Oriental history.

Of those who have occupied themselves with modern history, some indeed have written with a view mainly to the construction of a picturesque narrative; but mixed with these there has been an increasing number of workers whose aims have been chiefly scientific. An accomplished teacher, with a few advanced students, has published essays upon Anglo-Saxon law. Several Boston lawyers have published important studies in the history of English law. Here a historical scholar devotes himself to the study of the merchant-guild, or meditates the vexed subject of early landholding among the Germans; there another illustrates the history of the Prussian state. Another labors upon the history of sacerdotal celibacy, benefit of clergy, ordeal, and wager of battle. All this would have seemed very dry to the last generation; but the most judicious of the moderns see in it a hopeful sign for the future of the science, a sign that what work is done among us in European history hereafter will be, in increasing proportion, solid in construction and addressed not unsuccessfully to superior and specialized intelligence.

We have been speaking of departments of historical work in America upon which the war had little effect, and in whose development it could only arbitrarily be taken as a dividing point. But with work upon our own history, which has occupied an increasing proportion of our attention, it is otherwise. Its character has been profoundly affected by that great conflict. Not that we have yet had the best that we shall have in the way of books on the conflict itself. We have had excellent pieces of military history, a host of regimental histories and war articles. But the books which have attempted to deal with its political aspects have been, with a few exceptions like that of Mr. Alexander Stephens, hopelessly unfair, full of crude assumption, impervious to argument. The remedy for all these things will be the coming forward of the younger generation, whose motive for studying the war is not that of personal participation.

But the mental effects have extended far

more widely than this, far more widely than the whole field of history, in fact. The literature, the art indeed, of the United States can never again be like what it was before the civil war. It was not simply that the government became more firmly consolidated, the people more closely bound together. The nation emerged from that terrible struggle adult and mature. It was able to look upon itself and the world around it, its past and its future, at once with more sobriety and discrimination, and with a heightened self-respect, born of the sense that great achievements and sacrifices for inspiring causes had vindicated to it a right to independent views. Colonial attitudes of thought ceased, as colonial attitudes in politics had ceased after the war of 1812. National sensitiveness to condescending criticism from Europeans lost its acuteness; we began to feel, not in vanity, but in sobriety, that now we were as worthy as they. We began to look at our characteristics and modes of life with an externality of view unknown to the preceding generation. It was possible for the international novelist to arise, — that is, the novelist, to whom the American is not undoubtedly the greatest of all human types, but simply one human type among several, all alike to be exhibited with intelligent candor. Mr. Howells's voice, speaking to the American of forty years ago, would have been the voice of one crying in the wilderness, — a wilderness of vociferous panegyric upon all things American, whose very vociferousness betrayed a latent uneasiness. The development of our architecture, the gradual abandonment of Gothic and Renaissance styles for earlier styles, plainer, more Roman, more suited to the genius of a practical people, is another illustration. For the first time in our history we have become a self-reliant nation.

In the domain of American history, the change has taken effect in two directions or modes. In the first place, we have become more critical and discriminating, have learned more nearly to look upon the course of American history with an impartial eye, from the standpoint of an outsider. In the second place, there has ensued a broadening of the field of investigation and work, that its scope may correspond to the scheme of things in America, to the configuration of actual affairs. We are no longer content to adopt the same plans of distribution of attention to different phases of history which has seemed proper to European historians. Our writers recognize, consciously or unconsciously, that here the elements of life have been mixed in different proportions, and that history should conform to these different proportions as equally valid and worthy of observance.

To take at once one of the most important illustrations of this, one of the most vital differences between European history and that of the United States. It seems to be a fact that the scope of statesmanship, the influence of great individuals upon the general life, has been far less extensive here than there. It is certain to be so in new countries; in them Nature is supreme. Why was it that, while Greece itself was producing statesmen, the colonial Greeks of Sicily produced none? Simply because the abundance of Nature left no field for them. In modern Europe the pressure of population upon the means of subsistence, and all the difficulties which beset the general life wherever the gifts of Nature are not superabundant for the needs of man, have raised such problems for man to cope with, such tasks for the forces of human intelligence, as have necessarily evoked great administrative statesmen.

But with us it has not been so. Just as our national housekeeping has not needed, and therefore has not developed, the scientific financial methods of burdened Europe, the vastness of our national resources solving of itself every problem, so in general Nature has managed for us, and economic and other conditions have with peculiar completeness shaped our course. The governmental ideas which have been represented by the Straffords, the Richelieus, the Turgots, the Pitts, the Bismarcks of the old world (I do not mean ideas of absolutism, but ideas of dominant influence of great intellects upon national destinies), have been alien to America. Once, indeed, the effort was made to apply to America the methods of European administrative statesmanship. That is, if I am not mistaken, the essence of the Federalist experiment, more deeply its characteristic than any phase of its attitude towards the American Constitution. And why did the Federalist experiment break down? Simply because of those forces which the Hebrew war song indicates when it declares that the stars in their courses fought against Sisera. Nature would rule. With the advent of Jeffersonian democracy, the reins were thrown upon her neck; and from that time to this the field of influence of natural conditions upon our national destiny has been peculiarly great, the field of influence of great individuals far smaller than in the Old World. All this imposes upon our historical scholars a duty to which they have been far more disposed to conform since the attainment of a firmer national self-respect. They do not properly reflect the life that they seek to reflect if they write solely of individual persons or groups of persons and their conscious efforts; they must cease blindly to follow European schemes, and study economic and natural conditions and developments, the unintended growth of institutions and modes of life, the unconscious movements and changes of masses of men.

That this need of emancipation from the traditions and conventions of European historiography has been making itself felt, consciously or unconsciously, is plain to any one who surveys the historical literature of our day. Never was there a time in America when so great a proportion of the best historical work was devoted to the subject of the history of institutions and economics. One writes of the history of finance; another, of the fortunes of institutions transplanted westward, and the genesis of governmental ideas among the lawless frontiersmen; another, of the history of coöperation; still another, of movements of migratory population, and the influence of German or other national elements absorbed into our mass. The magazine writers give us series of articles on colonial manners and customs rather than on colonial wars. One writer even attempts the difficult task of writing a general history of our people. The historical publications of our universities are mostly devoted to the history of institutions and economics. Forty years ago, a man might write on the diplomacy of the American Revolution; nowadays, he is much more likely to write on the history of the produce exchange, or government land-grants for railways, or education. Monographs in the field of sociological history or on special topics of the history of civilization are the characteristic feature of our present historical literature.

One field indeed, whose cultivation would

naturally go along with these, is not yet receiving adequate attention, the study, namely, of the thought or inner life of our nation, of public opinion, of popular movements, political and other. It is not that we have no one corresponding to M. Renan; for the union of so subtle and profound an insight, so delicate and sympathetic an appreciation, and so exquisite a style, is not to be expected in a raw and youthful nation, and indeed has scarcely appeared before in any nation. But it is a matter of surprise that, with the exception of a few such books as Mr. Royce's "California," there seems but little tendency to the cultivation of that branch of history which may best be described as the study of the development of national psychology. But perhaps this will come in time.

This has been spoken of as the most important tendency of the historical writing of America to-day, not because its votaries or its productions are numerically in a majority, for that may very likely not be the case, but because of the belief that it is intrinsically the strongest tendency, and has the future with it. It is dangerous to prophesy; but there are good reasons why such a prophecy

may not be too audacious. The history of
every science is in some degree conditioned
by the natural course of things in the world
at large; but it appears true, and will perhaps
even have been shown by these papers,
that this is in a peculiar degree the case
with the science of history. Views of the
past, and ways of looking at it, change with
the changing complexion of the present.
But it is always found that the actual march
of affairs is far in advance of its expression
in literary theory and literary practice.
Democracy had for some time been established
among us before the poetry of democracy
arose. The world changes, but our
view of it does not change so fast; only with
great effort can it be kept up to date, so to
speak. Accordingly, it may be possible to
discern in the face of things at present
something which may be relied on to shape
in part the historical science of the immediate
future. Those characteristics of American
existence which have been mentioned
seem deeply rooted, permanent, essential;
therefore it is likely that the adjustment of
the sphere of our historical writing into conformity
with the actual facts, relations, and
proportions of our national existence will go

on to still further completeness, and that this tendency affords some presage as to its predominant qualities in the immediate future, — qualities catholic and philosophical, and contributory rather to historical science than to historical literature.

Of course not everything is sharing, or is likely to share, in this onward current. In particular, the tendencies of many of our numerous local historical societies form a counter-current, or, better, an eddy, in which chips of ancient timber float placidly round and round in the same little circle, quite unaffected by any general currents whatever. Most of them are very useful, and those of the West, at any rate, seem to be exceedingly active. But, with a few bright exceptions, our older historical societies seem a little inaccessible to new ideas, and more than a little wedded to tradition. The thought of touching anything that occurred since the Revolution, that is, of having anything to do with the most important part of our history, seems seldom to occur to them. Indeed, it is good fortune if the really active members are not absorbed exclusively in the study of the early voyages and discoveries, or of the Indians, the two subjects most remote from the present affairs of the United States, and therefore great favorites.

It is not likely that the more popular sort of books will change greatly in any short time. The voluminous and copiously illustrated county and city histories, with which swift and enterprising compilers from time to time present us, will probably not be much affected. Provided adequate attention has been given to the essential parts of their work, the advertisements of important industries and the engravings of prominent citizens, it will not be worth while to alter a method which has hitherto served well enough the main purpose of such publications. Indeed, it is to be expected that a large number of even the books of leading importance, whose ideas gradually filter into the popular books and school text-books, will continue to be constructed in accordance with the plans traditional to the art. This, provided it is not done from mere blindness or imperviousness to new ideas, will not be regretted. No one quarrels with Mr. Henry Adams for confining his brilliant and instructive books mainly to the political and constitutional history of the periods which they treat, or with Mr. Schouler for a similar course. There is still a vast work remaining to be done in our political history pure and simple. The main object is not the cessation of all former varieties of work, but the addition of numberless new ones, and the pervasion of all with more modern and catholic ideas.

But now as to the channels through which the historical movement of the present time goes on, and those likely to be used in the immediate future. With but a few exceptions, the local historical societies are not likely to be of great use in this way. Historical scholars of a modern spirit are no longer much in the habit of using their transactions as media of communication with the world. The newly founded American Historical Association, on the other hand, may be put to very good uses. The founding of that society was a most hopeful sign. If adequately supported by the real workers, it may prove of signal benefit to the progress of the science in the future. The scope of its publications is broad and national. Its connections with the government will enable it to publish still more, and out of it may grow a Historical Manuscripts Commission, which would be likely to accomplish as much for history among us as the prototype has accomplished in England. Whether through this channel or not, the government will not probably much longer delay to engage in some scheme of historical publication. Several state governments are now carrying out such enterprises.

Of our few historical magazines, most are the organs of one or another of the local societies; and of the more general ones it is hard to speak with much patience. The fault lies mostly with the general public, who have not yet begun to care much for good historical work. Indeed, for any essay in the domain of European history it is scarcely possible to think of any American outlet, now that our old-fashioned reviews have become extinct or worse. As for American history, what appears in the historical magazines is mostly of a very popular sort; it is only on condition of their maintaining such a composition that the " intelligent public " allows them to continue to exist at all. Meanwhile, however, the great literary magazines have opened their columns to series of good popular articles upon colonial or revolutionary history, or even the general or the more recent history of the United States, the last and apparently the most successful of such ventures being the war articles of "The Century" magazine. Very likely this indicates, or may succeed in creating, a more general interest in history among the unprofessional. Meanwhile, the scientific workers may find an avenue of publication through the hospitable columns of the new "English Historical Review," since the prospect of having one of their own is exceedingly remote.

A method of historical publication much in vogue among us at present is that of putting forth a series of volumes by separate authors upon kindred subjects. We have had a series of "Campaigns of the Civil War," a series of "Lesser Wars of the United States," with some others, and, perhaps more conspicuous to the public eye, the "American Statesmen" series and the series on "American Commonwealths." The plan has its advantages and its defects. From the point of view of the publisher, it is eminently well-conceived. Greater attention is drawn to individual pieces of work when thus collected; greater interest is excited in the general subject when a mass of work upon it is presented. To some extent, the interests of the publishing business and of historical scholarship are identical. Whatever increases the audience and the influence of good work must be welcomed by the scholar. But it must not be forgotten — and some of the volumes on "American Statesmen" and "American Commonwealths" are illustrations of the fact — that, in a series of this sort, the good books bolster up the poor ones, and gain them a factitious repute and power. At the same time, the best books suffer from the general average, seldom acquiring more weight than their fraction of the collective weight of the series, nor as much as might accrue to them as independent publications. Another result is, that all the kindred subjects therein comprised, however various in many characteristics, are bound down to the same uniform fullness and style of treatment. If Alexander Hamilton is to have a volume of three hundred pages sextodecimo, so must Gouverneur Morris. Statesman A, whose life was spent in executive affairs, may be treated differently from Statesman B, who spent his life on the bench, but he will not be treated with anything like so strong a difference as the facts demand. If, as Mr. Bagehot says, "the genius of great affairs abhors nicety of division," still more does it abhor equality of division; and their treatment should correspond to their genius.

It is well worth while to take such considerations into account in any survey of our present state and prospects, because a tendency to more organization of historical work is just now very marked. It is not simply a result of that progression towards equality, that fading of individual saliency, which we have before noted. It is a tendency peculiarly American. A nation singularly devoted to business has transferred to the fields of literature and science the habits of business management. We educate by correspondence, we facilitate literary work by ingenious mechanical devices, we catalogue and systematize. No nation in the world is so addicted to bibliography and indexing. The English still, as frequently as not, publish books without indexes; the American who does such a thing is at once denounced by our reviewers as ripe for any atrocity. To say nothing of smaller bibliographies, Sabin's great dictionary of "Americana" already extends to about twoscore volumes, and will, when completed, embrace as many as a hundred thousand titles.

But we are going further in the organization of historical work, even to the writing of histories by organized forces, or by coöperation. An excellent instance is the preparation of a most extensive history of the Pacific Coast by the staff of trained assistants employed by a wealthy, able, and enthusiastic Californian historian, Mr. H. H. Bancroft. Retiring from the publishing business with great wealth, Mr. Bancroft has employed the energy and the methods of a business man in the collection, digestion, and presentation of materials. First, a great library has been collected, including all obtainable books bearing at all upon the history of Central America, Mexico, California, Utah, Oregon, British Columbia, and Alaska. Thousands of Mexican and Californian pamphlets have been gathered, and files of hundreds of newspapers from all parts of the Pacific Coast. Numerous valuable manuscripts have fallen into the collector's hands, and enormous masses of manuscript copies of state records and mission archives have been made specially for the library by his secretaries. Old pioneers still surviving have been visited, and their recollections taken down at great length. A Russian assistant was sent to Alaska to copy the government records there. Half a dozen Spanish ones have done similar work. From twelve to twenty accomplished linguists, we are told, have been constantly employed in Mr. Bancroft's service since 1869. Secretaries have all this time been reading, translating, summarizing, cataloguing, and indexing the whole collection.

The result, attained at the cost of half a million dollars, is a mass of systematized information, such as must make the users and the desirers of historical materials elsewhere deeply envious, and for the collection of which, under ordinary methods, even an antediluvian lifetime would scarcely suffice a historian. The highest praise must be given to the zeal for research, the public spirit, and the enterprise and care which have presided over the formation of this priceless collection. But when it comes to writing history by this same method, some reserves are necessarily suggested to the mind. Mr. Bancroft has prepared from these materials, and published, a gigantic " History of the Pacific States of America," in thirty-four unusually large volumes. It is obvious that a work of such magnitude, carried through in so few years, could not possibly be written by a single hand. In fact, the books were first written by the various members of the cohort of assistants, and the person whose name they bear has simply revised, as a sort of managing editor, the productions of this highly-organized staff. Valuable as the work proves to be, some of the faults of such a plan are evident. There can be no fixing of responsibility. No one knows whom to criticise. No one can know whether the authority of this or that part of the book, or of the whole, should be much or little. Moreover, there is less likelihood, under such a system, of the best historical criticism, the most skillful sifting of the evidence thus elaborately collected. But all this is on the supposition that the main object of historical composition is correctness of detail, that a book is perfect if none of its information is erroneous; a supposition by no means to be admitted. To any one who has any conception of the use of the higher powers, the rarer qualities of the mind, in historical composition, it will be plain that no really great history can be written by the methods of the "literary bureau," by hiring a force of assistants and seeing that they do it. It may almost be said that the historian, like the poet, is born, not made; but if he is made, he is not made by machinery.

Such dangers as have been above noted must always, in greater or less degree, attend work prepared by these or similar methods. It is important to observe this, because one sees, in this country so devoted to organization, a growing tendency toward the production of historical work in such ways, the application to it of the economic principle and method of division of labor. A far greater amount of work can thus be put forth, and, what perhaps is quite as important, can be put forth in such a way as greatly to increase its force upon the world; for work so combined and systematized with other work is not in danger of being lost or ineffectual, as are, for instance, the dissertations so ingeniously concealed in German university and school programmes. But it is well to remember that with these advantages there are some serious drawbacks. Good work of the second class, and great amounts of it, can thus be done; good work of the first class cannot. The tale of Pegasus in harness has this meaning, that the finest qualities of the human mind cannot be thus systematized. The highest intellects are not at the service of the hirers of clerks, are not to be made cogs or wheels in a history-producing machine.

By far the most noteworthy of our cooperative histories is the "Narrative and Critical History of America," edited by Mr. Justin Winsor. With its chapters of historical narrative by our most learned and able historical scholars, each writing upon his own special field, and with its critical essays upon the sources of information, it seems without doubt to be the most important and useful contribution ever yet made to American historical science. It splendidly sums up the historical labors of a century. And, by the way, consisting so largely as it does of a bibliographical record of what has been done, the proportion between its parts affords a striking indication of the relative amounts of work which Americans have expended on different portions of American history. It has taken four volumes to set forth the results achieved in our colonial and revolutionary history, while a single volume is thought to suffice for the period from 1789 to 1850. Another editor might divide the work somewhat differently; but the fact remains that we have expended much more labor on the earlier than on the later period of our history. Perhaps new nations have a passion for the study of origins; or perhaps even those who write history enjoy an interesting story, and find more such in colonial history than in later times. The disproportion indicated is a necessary incident to the scheme of the work. There are also, it should be noted, other limitations which must to some extent beset all cooperative or monographic histories alike. Stretched on the Procrustean bed of uniform requirements in respect to extensiveness and general method of treatment, the authors can present only those things which they have in common, — abundant and correct information, and acute historical criticism. Many of the finer qualities of the individual mind are likely to evaporate in the process; much of what is most valuable in individual views and conceptions of history will find no place for itself. No one who appreciates these will readily assent to the assertion, in the prospectus to the "Narrative and Critical History," that, "when the superiority of the coöperative method is fully understood, the individual historian, if he ventures forth at all, will be read for entertainment rather than profit."

And now as to the agents by whom historical science is to be furthered. Here, also, the present enables us to judge somewhat of the future. It is not probable that the advance-guard of our army will be led by the ruling members of the various local historical societies. Nor, on the other hand, will much be done by the class of professionally literary men. At New York, we are assured, there is now a literary centre, and in and near it a literary class; and lest the public should lose sight of the fact, each of our great magazines has at times an article by some one of the number in which the rest are commemorated, each star being catalogued by these prompt astronomers as soon as it succeeds in getting at all above the horizon. But with these complacent Augustans, literature appears to be mostly a branch of journalism, and history has little to expect from them. No doubt their school surpasses in breadth and the cosmopolitan quality that which forty years ago had its centre in Boston, but it is as much inferior in scholarship as it is in dignity. The local antiquaries, the professionally literary men, and the men of wealth and leisure devoted to study, will no doubt continue to write historical books. But an increasing proportion of the annual product now comes from the teachers of history in universities and colleges, and the signs are that the immediate future belongs to the professorial class.

The change is more significant than may at first be seen. Its meaning will appear if we bear in mind that want of early training in the technique of historical research and composition which has been already spoken of as characteristic of American historians hitherto. The increasing identification of the writing and the teaching classes may be relied on to remove this obstacle to progress. The next generation will have served an apprenticeship under men who write; and the superior finish, the improvement in scholarly method, which have been so much needed, will be one of the results. Already, increasing numbers of special students of history are frequenting those universities which afford graduate instruction, and if the annual production of books and other publications giving evidence of scientific training and of high ideals of historical scholarship is still small, it is visibly increasing.

Thus we have traced the development of our science from its half-conscious infancy down to the present time, and perhaps a little way into the future. It cannot truly be said that it has yet reached anything like maturity, but it is in a vigorous though raw adolescence.

www.ingramcontent.com/pod-product-compliance
Lightning Source LLC
Chambersburg PA
CBHW031456160426
43195CB00010BB/994